Celebrating Christmas

TRADITIONS, TALES & TRUTHS

J.JOHN

ILLUSTRATED BY LISA ALDERSON

Design Management by Jeni Child

Cover Design and Illustrations by Lisa Alderson

Original Cover Concept and Design by Andy Gray

Print Management by Verité CM Ltd

www.veritecm.com

Printed in the UK

CONTENTS

PREFACE

Christmas is a delightful kaleidoscope: a cheerful, colourful and frequently clashing blend of sounds, lights and images. Santa Claus rubs shoulders with shepherds, there's holly in the stable, the kings Wenceslas and Herod sit on adjacent thrones and camels plod along in the snow.

Christmas is bright but also, well, *confusing*. Tightly interwoven with the biblical story that is the foundation of Christmas are medieval tales, Victorian traditions and modern embellishments, few of which fit comfortably together. In one of the season's favourite films, *Love Actually*, a little girl announces that she'll be playing 'first lobster' in her school's nativity play. 'There was more than one lobster present at the birth of Jesus?' her mother asks.

In fact, what we have merging and intertangled at this season are three separate things: the religious Christmas with its Christian truths; the social Christmas with its traditions of food and family gatherings; and the 'commodity Christmas'. So when someone says, 'I love (or loathe) Christmas,' it is important to ask exactly what *type* of Christmas they are referring to. Indeed, it's worth asking yourself what sort of Christmas you want.

So this is an A to Z book that seeks to work through many of these traditions, tales and truths.

I hope it will help you have a deeper, richer and truer Christmas.

I thank the God who, unable to make himself bigger to impress us, instead made himself smaller to attract us.

Merry Christmas and peace be with you.

J. John

ADVENT

The run-up to Christmas is considered by the church as the season of Advent, from the Latin '*Adventus*', or 'coming'. Advent is a time of preparation, lasting four weeks, which, while it should always involve reflection, sometimes involves fasting. The first mention of an 'Advent Season' was at the Council of Tours in 567, when a fast for monks in December was recorded. At the close of the 6th century, Gregory the Great of Rome made a rule of fasting for the four Sundays in Advent and soon the season became widely practised throughout the church.

In the past, Advent fasting could be substantial, with people avoiding such things as meat, dairy produce, fish, wine and oil. Today Advent fasting is often less severe, perhaps simply avoiding consuming things such as alcohol and chocolate. Fasting or not, Advent is valuable as a season of consideration and reflection; particularly about the universal need for us all to be rescued by God.

One aspect of Advent that should not be overlooked is the fact that, in Christian thinking, it is a season that looks not simply back to Jesus' first coming in **Bethlehem**, but also forward to his final coming in his Second Advent at the end of history that will be unmistakable and inescapable.

In Advent the feast of Christmas is always on the horizon and there is an element of counting down to the great day. So, in many churches, the four Sundays before Christmas are celebrated by successively lighting four candles. For many people, especially those with children, the drawing near of Christmas is marked by the **Advent calendar**.

One problem with Advent today is that it has become a season where the demands of practical preparation can displace any spiritual reflection. For many people – particularly, I fear, mothers – the run up to Christmas is a stressful season with dilemmas and decisions over how to manage the looming festive season. Contrary to what some individuals in a family can imagine, the successful Christmas does not just happen. It involves detailed planning on buying presents, reducing the Christmas card list, drafting a summary of the year, ordering the turkey, organising dinner parties and other essential matters of who, where, when, what and how.

Ironically, and quite unintentionally, the way that commercialism and consumerism, preparation and panic have invaded the Advent season points to why we need a truer, deeper Christmas. Unless your festivities have a framework to give them shape and a focus to direct them, then other pressures – louder, more appealing and more urgent – will inevitably squeeze the season out of shape. Looking towards Christmas at Advent we need to keep 'the main thing the main thing'. If we don't, there is the danger of a festival where we are either continually operating in crisis-management mode or where secondary matters have taken centre stage and, in a phrase, the wrapping paper is getting more attention than the gift.

The church has always seen Advent as being not just about the first and second comings of **Christ**, but also about a third. With the first we look back to the historical nativity in Bethlehem. With the second we look forward to the second coming sometime in the future. With the third we look at ourselves: the arrival of Christ into our own lives. In the much-loved **carol** 'O Little Town of Bethlehem' there is an important set of lines:

> No ear may hear his coming,
> But in this world of sin,
> Where meek souls will receive him, still
> The dear Christ enters in.

It's all very well believing in Christ and his birth but it's important not to miss the vital element of personally receiving him as our own Saviour and Lord.

ADVENT CALENDAR

The most obvious expression of the countdown to Christmas today is the Advent calendar, a card with a flap for each day of the season, revealing something underneath. This is one of many aspects of our Christmas celebration.

When Advent calendars originated some two hundred years ago, they were religious, with each window revealing a Bible verse or an image depicting an aspect of the Christmas story. Later came the calendars with a small chocolate or sweet underneath. With the rise of the 'commercial Christmas', Advent calendars have become increasingly detached from anything to do with the origins of Christmas.

ANNUNCIATION

The Annunciation refers to the account of the **angel** Gabriel's visit to Mary in which he announces that she will give birth to a son, Jesus. We read about it in Luke's gospel **(1:26-38)**. The celebration of the Annunciation occurs nine months before Christmas on 25th March. Nevertheless, the Annunciation tends to get brought into the Christmas celebrations because it is a key part of the nativity story.

In Luke we read that God sent Gabriel to Nazareth, to Mary, a virgin who was already pledged to be married to Joseph, a man who is a descendant of David. The angel announced (hence the 'Annunciation') that Mary was a

woman favoured by God, that he was with her and she
would conceive and give birth to a son who would be
called Jesus. Gabriel then outlines who this son will be.
He will be very great and called 'Son of the Most High',
'the Lord God will give him the throne of his ancestor
David', he will reign over God's people Israel forever
and his kingdom will never end.

There's a lot going on here:

- The infant is to be called Jesus, which in Hebrew means
  'the Lord saves', that the child is going to be some sort
  of saviour, deliverer or rescuer.

- The child is going to be very great.

- He will be called 'the Son of the Most High'. It's important
  to note that the term 'son' here does not refer to any sort
  of biological relationship but rather to the idea of authority;
  like an heir to the throne, this Jesus will act with the
  authority of God himself.

- The child is going to sit on the throne of his ancestor
  David. This is a reference to the great promise to
  David (2 Samuel 7:1-17, Isaiah 9:7) that he would have
  a descendant who would be King over God's people
  and who would be even greater than he was. This
  figure – the 'Son of David' – is the **Messiah** or **Christ**.

- Unlike David, or his son Solomon, Jesus' reign and his
  kingdom will never end.

In other words, all the great themes of the Christian
gospel are here announced in summary. However, at this

point Mary is, quite understandably, less preoccupied with this awesome theology than with one very practical aspect: she is a virgin. Not only do virgins not conceive but in a rural Middle Eastern culture, pregnancy outside marriage is a matter of immorality that brings with it an intense shame on both the individual and her community that must be punished, as in the appalling and dishonourable 'honour killings' that still occur today.

Significantly, Mary is one of the few people in the Bible who asks a question of an angel and is granted an explanation. Gabriel says that the Holy Spirit will come upon her, God's power will overshadow her, and the baby that will be born will be called 'holy' and 'the Son of God'. Presumably to encourage her to believe what must seem unbelievable, the angel reveals to Mary that her relative **Elizabeth** has become pregnant. The dialogue ends with Mary's wonderful and faith-filled response, 'I am the Lord's servant, may all you have said come true.'

BAUBLES

A bauble is any sort of decorative glass, plastic, metal or even wooden ball that we put on a **Christmas tree**.

The earliest decorated trees seem to have been adorned with pastries, apples, **nuts** and **candy canes**. Glass baubles originated in Germany in the 16th century and soon became popular there. In the 19th century the technique of applying a silver film was perfected to create the modern glittering spheres that act as the jewellery of the Christmas tree.

Baubles were one of many Continental Christmas traditions popularised in Britain by Queen Victoria and her husband Albert. Glass baubles continued to grow in popularity in the 20th century but after the Second World War began to be replaced by high-quality plastic baubles, which had the virtue of being more resistant to breakage.

Christmas baubles may be deeply prized. Indeed, in some households Christmas decorations may even have been handed on from previous generations, something that gives them a symbolic value. As such they contribute to one of the most valuable aspects of Christmas: in an age of relentless innovation they provide a link back, over many years, to our past.

BELLS

Bells are associated with Christmas in various ways. The most obvious and traditional link has been through the use of church bells to summon people to worship, something that may go back to Roman times.

Until personal clocks and watches became widespread in the mid-19th century, it was the chiming of the church bell that set the time for a community. Indeed, bells did more than that. By ringing and tolling in different ways they spoke of the celebration of a wedding, the warning of war and the sad solemnity of a funeral.

Bells, especially church bells, retain an association with Christmas. In Scandinavia, bells still ring at 5pm on Christmas Eve to signal that Christmas has started and people can leave work.

Bells have found their way into many Christmas songs and carols. Although 'Jingle Bells' has become part of Christmas tradition, it was originally published in the USA in 1857 for Thanksgiving.

The carol 'Ding Dong! Merrily on High' is perhaps the most prominent in its reference to bells with its joyful first verse:

Ding dong! merrily on high
In heav'n the bells are ringing
Ding dong! verily the sky
Is riv'n with angel singing
Gloria, Hosanna in excelsis

Perhaps the most thoughtful reference to Christmas bells comes in 'I Heard the Bells on Christmas Day'. It is based on a poem written by Henry Wadsworth Longfellow in 1863. Longfellow, a famous poet, had suffered much personal sadness and was greatly grieved by the American Civil War then tearing apart his nation. The poem – and the carol – laments the rise of hate and the mockery of peace. Nevertheless, the final two verses are optimistic and the carol ends in a most positive way with a quotation of the angels' message to the shepherds.

And in despair I bowed my head;
'There is no peace on earth,' I said;
'For hate is strong,
And mocks the song
Of peace on earth, good-will to men!'

Then pealed the bells more loud and deep:
'God is not dead, nor doth he sleep;
The Wrong shall fail,
The Right prevail,
With peace on earth, good-will to men.'

It's not hard to look around the world and realise the need for this sort of hope today. We always need reminding that at the heart of Christmas lies the news of the birth of Jesus and, in that, the coming of hope into the darkness of this world.

BETHLEHEM

Bethlehem, whose name comes from the Hebrew '*Bayt laḥm*' or 'house of bread', plays a significant part in the Old Testament. Lying in the territory of the biblical tribe of Judah, it was the hometown of David, the shepherd boy who rose to become the warrior king who founded a united Israel around 1000 BC. David's reign – along with his son Solomon – was long looked back on as Israel's golden age, particularly as the Jewish people found themselves under a succession of brutal rulers. Yet David was not simply a figure of history. The Bible records that God promised him a dynasty and that, one day, one of his descendants would be an even greater king. This became the basis of the belief in the long-awaited **Messiah**; the deliverer who would rescue God's people and overthrow all their enemies. The prophet Micah wrote:

> But you, Bethlehem Ephrathah, though you are small among the clans of Judah, out of you will come for me one who will be ruler over Israel, whose origins are from of old, from ancient times. (Micah 5:2)

By New Testament times, Bethlehem appears to have become an almost insignificant place, only some 8 kilometres (5 miles) away in Jerusalem.

Very early on, the Christian church recognised the significance of Bethlehem, and churches and monuments were built there to celebrate the birthplace of Jesus.

BOXING DAY

In many countries 26th December is celebrated as a holiday, and in some it still retains Christian significance as Saint Stephen's Day, the second day of the Christmas festival, commemorating Stephen, the first Christian martyr (Acts 7:54-60).

In Britain, 26th December is termed Boxing Day. The origin of the name reflects the fact that on this day, gifts were given to the poor; money was put in a box at church, which was opened after Christmas to be shared among local people. Workers and apprentices had pottery boxes, which they would take to their masters' customers and ask for money. On Boxing Day the pottery boxes were smashed and the money spent on food and drink. The 26th was made an official holiday in 1871, apparently to allow servants, who would have been waiting on their masters and mistresses on Christmas Day, an opportunity to visit their own families.

One element of the increasing commercialisation of the Christmas period has been the fact that, in Britain at least, many sales start on Boxing Day and are notoriously packed. The day is also traditionally marked by indigestion and the eating of left-over remains from the Christmas lunch: the infamous cold-turkey sandwich!

BRUSSELS SPROUTS

Brussels sprouts are members of the cabbage family, the individual sprouts growing in bunches of twenty to forty on the stem of a plant. Ironically, considering the unfortunate reputation of sprouts, they are one of the very few ingredients in Christmas Day foods that get the approval of dietitians. Low in fat and, if not overboiled, high in antioxidants, sprouts are packed full of vitamin C, folic acid, beta carotene, vitamin E and iron.

Brussels sprouts were named after the capital of Belgium, where they may have been cultivated for many centuries.

Personally, I can manage a few, carefully cooked, once a year on Christmas Day. And no more!

CAESAR AUGUSTUS

Those unfamiliar with the nativity story often find themselves struck by its mention of Caesar Augustus. In an age where fantasy rules, particularly at the cinema box office, the name of one of the most distinguished of Roman Caesars in the Bible text is a reminder that this tale makes a claim to be fact rather than fiction.

Augustus is one of the big figures of Roman history. Born in 63 BC and originally called Octavian, he was Julius Caesar's great-nephew and his adopted heir. When Julius Caesar was assassinated, he took over and proved so successful that he was renamed 'Augustus', meaning 'venerable' or 'esteemed'. He ruled in Rome for over fifty years with considerable success, overseeing the expansion of the empire around the Mediterranean and creating a dynasty that was to last for another century. He was the first Roman emperor and died in AD 14. He was succeeded by his adopted son Tiberius, the figure whom Jesus refers to as 'Caesar'.

When Jesus was born, Augustus was the most powerful leader in the known world. Luke's gospel records how Augustus issued a decree that a census be taken of the entire Roman world, forcing Joseph and Mary to travel to **Bethlehem**, Joseph's ancestral home.

The reference to Caesar Augustus anchors the birth of **Christ** into global history. Yet, as is so often the case with the gospels, there is a lot more going on than just facts. So, for instance, there is here an enormous and thought-provoking contrast. On the one hand we have the mighty figure of the all-powerful Emperor of Rome, the greatest ruler the world had seen, here commanding the movement of faraway people. On the other hand we see the apparently insignificant figures of Joseph and Mary moved around at the will of Roman bureaucracy and resorting to staying in an animal shed for the birth of their baby. Yet, as Luke will emphasise both in his gospel and in its sequel the Book of Acts, news of this baby and his identity will challenge the Roman Empire.

There is a delightful and thought-provoking irony here that Caesar Augustus is now known only to historians, while the infant born in poverty is worshipped as God by at least a third of the world's population. It's the ultimate in role reversals.

CANDLEMAS

Although Candlemas – 2nd February – is not part of Christmas, it is linked with it. Technically the 'Feast of the Presentation of Jesus Christ' or the 'Feast of the Purification of the Blessed Virgin Mary', it is a Christian festival commemorating the presentation of the baby Jesus at the temple.

The background to the presentation of Jesus in the temple is that the law of the Old Testament required that, after the birth of a baby, a woman had to be 'purified' at the temple. This involved the offering of a lamb, if the family was wealthy, or a pigeon or a dove if it wasn't. This was to be done forty days after a boy's birth and thirty-three days after his circumcision. So taking the birth of Jesus as 25th December, this takes us to 2nd February.

We read of the presentation of Jesus in **Luke 2:22-40**, where the focus is not so much on the ceremony but on the encounter between the baby and Simeon and Anna, two aged and faithful figures who recognise the significance of the baby and make prophecies.

CANDY CANE

It's common at Christmas, especially in America, to encounter candy canes, traditionally white with red stripes and flavoured with peppermint, either as treats or as ornaments on a **Christmas tree**.

Like so many Christmas traditions, the origin of the candy cane is obscure. One legend is that in 1670, the choirmaster of Cologne Cathedral found himself irritated by the noise children made during Christmas services. To keep them quiet he ordered sugar sticks from a local candy maker and, when asked to justify this practice, had them made in the form of a shepherd's crook to remind the children of the shepherds visiting Jesus.

Candy canes became popular and spread across Europe. Like many European traditions they were taken to America by migrants and soon became part of American church culture. Eventually, candy canes became so linked with Christmas that they became an emblem of the season and found their way onto Christmas cards.

CAROLS

A distinguishing feature of Christmas is its special music. The word 'carol' comes from an Old French word *'carole'*, which referred to a popular circle dance accompanied by singing, and many of the carols that we sing have hints of the dance in their tunes. The Christian church dropped the dance element, but kept the melodies.

The earliest formal collection of carols, *Christmasse Carolles*, was published by the wonderfully named Wynkyn de Worde in 1521. Although different Protestant denominations were divided over the nature and importance of church music, they seem to have been united in excluding carols from church services. Nevertheless, sung outside the church,

in the pub, in the ploughed field and around the hearth, carols endured from generation to generation. In the 19th century there was a renewed interest in carols and many were rediscovered, translated and, with words more suitable for Victorian sensitivities, introduced into church worship.

A key event in the history of carols was the publication of a series of volumes from 1867 onwards entitled *Christmas Carols, New and Old* by the Reverend Henry Bramley and the celebrated Victorian composer Sir John Stainer. Eventually, running to a collection of some seventy carols, it included such modern favourites as 'The First Nowell', 'God Rest You Merry, Gentlemen', 'See Amid the Winter's Snow', 'Once In Royal David's City' and 'What Child Is This?'

It's interesting that we read in **Luke 2:20** that 'the shepherds returned, glorifying and praising God for all the things they had heard and seen'. I can make a safe guess that what they sang was rough, ready and joyful, and I think it would have had a good deal in common with carols.

CAROL SERVICE

The standard pattern for a carol service is to alternate carols with readings from the Bible that tell the nativity story. Frequently, a carol service occurs in a church setting lit by candles or, increasingly, their LED imitations.

The best-known, regularly repeated carol service is probably the Festival of Nine Lessons and Carols. The first version of this was devised in 1880 by the Reverend Edward Benson.

Benson created it for Truro Cathedral and started it at 10pm on Christmas Eve in the hope of getting men out of the pubs before they got too drunk. Benson's pattern was borrowed and revised in 1918 by Eric Milner-White for King's College, Cambridge, and made use of the King's College choir.

By all accounts the first occasion, held only weeks after the Armistice that ended the First World War, was a sombre event as the university took stock of the vast number of students and staff who had been killed. The BBC started broadcasting the service in 1928 and, except for 1930, it has been broadcast every year since. In the 1930s it began being broadcast worldwide on what was then the Overseas Service (later the BBC World Service) and continues to have a massive global audience, currently estimated to be several hundred million listeners.

The Festival of Nine Lessons and Carols from King's has become something of an anchor point for British expatriates (and others) who find themselves away from home at Christmas. From oil rigs to warships, tents to palaces, the equator to the poles, men and women – some who may not have been in a church for years – fall silent and listen, with nostalgia, as the unaccompanied solo treble chorister soars away with 'Once in Royal David's City'. Christmas, and all the memories it brings, has begun!

CHARITY

There is a long tradition of charity at Christmas. Charity is to give freely to those who are in need, such as the ill, poor or homeless. Yet it is also an emotion linked to that act: an expression of kindness, compassion or even love. At its best charity involves looking out from ourselves to others, shifting the focus of our life from our wants and own desires to those of others.

The word 'charity' originated as the 'Christian love of one's fellows'. It came into English, via French, from the Latin 'caritas', which was the translation of the Greek word 'agape'. 'Agape' is used in the New Testament (114 times!) for the highest form of love, which is an unconditional and often sacrificial love for those 'who do not deserve our love'. It is the love that God has for us and the love that any who know God through Jesus should have for others. It's discussed in 1 Corinthians 13, where Saint Paul writes a wonderful passage about the importance of 'agape' love, ending in verse 13 with the phrase in the Authorised Version of the Bible,

'And now abideth faith, hope, charity, these three; but the greatest of these is charity.' Here, as elsewhere, most modern Bible versions replace charity with 'love'.

Very briefly, we could say that Jesus *taught* the necessity of 'charity' or 'love', particularly in the so-called 'Sermon on the Mount' (Matthew chapters 5 to 7); for instance, in his ruling to 'love your neighbour as yourself'. He also *commanded* his followers to display it to each other (John 13:34). Perhaps above all, he *modelled* it in who he was. The New Testament is clear that Jesus was sent as a gift to us by God:

> For God so loved the world that he *gave* his one and only Son, that whoever believes in him shall not perish but have eternal life. (John 3:16)

In Jesus' earthly life, from cradle to cross, we see an act of love that involved an extraordinary sacrifice. As Jesus said himself in words that have echoed on through the ages:

> Greater love has no one than this: to lay down one's life for one's friends. (John 15:13)

So you can see that, even if it is not spelled out, Christmas commemorates God expressing his love to humanity. I don't think anybody knows when the tradition of giving gifts began but it fits well with the idea that, as we have received a gift from God, so we ought to give gifts to others. In the Middle Ages there were pressures in society for the well-off to open their doors to the less fortunate at Christmas and provide them with food and drink. A long tradition remains of charitable giving at Christmas through generous tipping, providing food hampers and handing out bonuses in pay packets.

An organisation specifically geared to helping the homeless at this time is Crisis at Christmas. Another opportunity for Christmas charity comes with those organisations that send gift-filled shoe boxes to children in need around the world – one organisation that has been doing this for years is Samaritan's Purse.

When the transformed Scrooge in **Charles Dickens'** *A Christmas Carol* realises that he needs to show charity, he does it with a tremendous exuberance.

Ultimately, the most important thing at Christmas is not what we gain but what we give.

CHRIST

The word 'Christ' comes from the Greek '*Christos*', which means 'someone who is anointed'. It is the word that replaces the important Hebrew word '**Messiah**' in the Greek translation of the Old Testament that was popular in the Jewish community around the Mediterranean at the time of Jesus.

In the Old Testament we read of three categories of individuals who, as a symbol of their divine authority, were anointed with oil: prophets, priests and kings.

At the time of the first Christmas the word 'Messiah' mainly had the sense of the great king or deliverer long promised by God, something that encouraged Jewish believers and troubled their Roman occupiers. So it is a title and you could say that if Jesus is a personal name, Christ is a title. The word 'Messiah' was important: for a Christian to say, 'I believe in Jesus Christ,' is to say, 'I believe that Jesus is the long-prophesied Messiah, the Saviour and Deliverer of the Jewish people and the world, sent by God.'

It's a big claim and much of what appears in the gospels is written to justify this claim. The gospel writer John ends his book with the following phrase:

> But these [things] are written that you may believe that Jesus is the Messiah, the Son of God, and that by believing you may have life in his name. (John 20:31)

If you want to pursue this further and read how Jesus was the Messiah or Christ and what this means, then I'd recommend the book *Jesus Christ – The Truth* that I wrote with Chris Walley.

Incidentally, in Greek the first letter of Christ is a *chi*, which looks like an X. There is a tradition that is at least 500 years old of abbreviating the word 'Christ' simply to X. In that sense 'Xmas' is a perfectly reasonable abbreviation for Christmas.

CHRISTINGLE

A Christingle is an orange pierced by cocktail sticks bearing sweets and capped with a candle but, in practice, the word can refer to a service in which such things are made.

In 1747 John de Wattville, a church minister in what is now modern Germany, wanted to find a new way of expressing the Christmas story to children. He gave each of them a candle tied with a red ribbon and asked them to light the candles at home and place them in their windows to show the light of **Christ** to those who passed by. The tradition evolved and was kept alive by the Moravian denomination and was adopted in the UK in the 1960s as a fundraising tool for the Children's Society of the Church of England, from where it spread.

The Christingle orange represents the world, and the lighted candle represents Christ, the Light of the world. The **nuts**, raisins and sweets on cocktail sticks around the candle represent God's goodness in supplying the fruits of the earth to human beings. The red paper, either around the base of the candle or around the orange, is a reminder of the blood of Christ shed for humanity on the cross.

CHRISTMAS CAKE

When it comes to Christmas foods, every country – and sometimes every family – has its own tradition. One longstanding and much-loved English ritual is that of making or buying a Christmas cake – a rich, moist fruit cake that is often covered in layers of marzipan, then icing, then seasonal decorations. The goal of a perfect Christmas cake is to make something that doesn't simply taste wonderful, but also looks magnificent. It competes for attention with the **Christmas dinner** as the highlight of Christmas and, for many people, cutting a slice of 'the cake' towards the end of Christmas Day is an essential part of the festivities.

A Christmas cake includes dried fruit, brandy, butter, sugar, eggs, flour and spices. One distinctive aspect of the Christmas cake is that it is made well in advance, with some cooks advocating that it be baked in November. Many Christmas cake experts suggest that having made it well in advance, you 'feed' the cake a tablespoon of alcohol every couple of weeks.

Christmas cake is claimed to have originated as 'plum porridge' and was used to end a fast on Christmas Eve. Over time this evolved down two paths: one to Christmas cake, the other to **Christmas pudding**.

CHRISTMAS CARDS

For most people, a key element of the Christmas season is the sending of greeting cards, something that is one of the great rituals of this time of the year.

The first commercial Christmas cards were created in 1843 by Sir Henry Cole, who had something of a vested interest as he had just introduced the 'penny post' to Britain, with its stamped letters allowing the cost of posting to be borne by the sender not the recipient. The first cards bore the words 'A Merry Christmas and a Happy New Year' and depicted three generations of a family raising a toast to the card's recipient. It's an interesting reflection of the times that the card bore images of the poor being helped in various ways.

With the development of printing techniques, high-quality colour cards became cheaper and soon the sending of cards was an essential part of the Christmas season. In fact, Christmas cards soon acquired a deep significance in defining who was, or who wasn't, part of your social circle.

Soon greetings cards evolved into different types, with a division between those that proclaimed the religious aspects of Christmas and those that avoided them. The former portrayed aspects of the Christmas story, such as the **crib scene**, the holy family and the **wise men**. The latter depicted candles, holly, **baubles** and **Christmas trees**, wintery **snow** scenes and **robins**, or even humorous depictions of **Santa**.

A CHRISTMAS CAROL

Of all the works of literature on Christmas, undoubtedly the most famous is the novel *A Christmas Carol* by **Charles Dickens**. Published in 1843 to enormous popular acclaim it has shaped how we imagine and practise Christmas today.

In his novel Dickens brought together three elements. The first was the ghost story, and the second a social criticism with its compassionate treatment of the poor. The final element is the idea of redemption; the idea of a bad man becoming a good one, which Dickens drew from Christianity.

The key figure in *A Christmas Carol* is Ebenezer Scrooge, a bitter old miser who loathes Christmas, believing it is 'a time for finding yourself a year older, and not an hour richer'.

Scrooge practises his belief, only grudgingly allowing his overworked and underpaid clerk Bob Cratchit to take **Christmas Day** off. However, on **Christmas Eve** Scrooge is visited by the ghost of a former business partner who tells him that, to show him the error of his ways, he will be visited by three spirits.

That night Scrooge is visited in turn by the Ghost of Christmas Past, the Ghost of Christmas Present, and the Ghost of Christmas Yet to Come, with each showing him the past, present and future consequences of his actions. The Ghost of Christmas Present shows him Bob Cratchit's family and, amongst them, his youngest son Tiny Tim, who is seriously ill. The Ghost of Christmas Yet to Come shows Scrooge his own miserably attended funeral.

Scrooge, now aware of the true impact of his outlook and actions, awakens on Christmas morning a changed man. He makes a big donation to a charity he'd rejected the previous day, sends a large turkey to the Cratchit home for Christmas dinner, and spends the afternoon at a Christmas party. The following day he gives Bob Cratchit a pay increase and begins to take care of Tiny Tim. Scrooge, now the very embodiment of 'the spirit of Christmas', treats everyone with kindness, generosity and compassion.

A Christmas Carol is a wonderful, heart-warming story. It is also extremely perceptive in its depiction of Scrooge as someone devoted only to himself and his money.

A Christmas Carol is important in that it helped create the Christmas season that we have today.

CHRISTMAS DAY

Christmas Day is the focal point of the festive period. Long celebrated on 25th December in most European and North American countries, it has 'gone global' in a big way and become one of the few days in the year when business and shopping industries fall silent across the world.

Christmas was celebrated in Rome on 25th December in AD 336. One reason for this date seems to be that it fell nine months after the Feast of the **Annunciation**, which was considered to be 25th March. The fact that 25th December was the solstice in the Roman Empire is doubtless significant. With days now visibly lasting longer, this was the feast of *Sol Invictus* – the 'unconquerable sun'. The church, pointing out that one of the terms for Jesus was 'the sun of righteousness' (a phrase found in **Malachi 4:2**, one of the Old Testament prophecies about the **Messiah**), changed the festival from the unconquerable sun to the unconquerable Son. By the 5th century, 25th December seems to have become the accepted date for Christmas.

Although celebrating Christmas is an ancient tradition, the name is less so. The first use of Christmas, *Cristes Maesse* – the Mass of **Christ** – occurs in Old English around 1000. Traditionally the church held Midnight Mass, commemorating the visitation of the **shepherds**, and the Day Mass, celebrating the coming of God's Son, Jesus Christ.

CHRISTMAS DECORATIONS

'Deck the hall with boughs of holly' is a reminder that before the **Christmas tree** became an indispensable element of the season, decorations for the **Twelve Days of Christmas** were garlands of holly, ivy and other evergreens.

Today, elaborate garlands of tinsel, fake greenery and ribbons, together with every conceivable kind of decoration – such as models of **carol** singers, **snow** globes, Christmas elves or polar bears – are on display in shops from early September onwards. Some homes are elaborately decorated, both inside and out, from the start of December.

Very early on in the history of the Christmas tree, decorations simply consisted of **nuts**, fruits, sweets, biscuits and ribbon bows. Many of the decorations were produced in the home. With time, candles were used and **tinsel** added to multiply the impression of light. **Baubles** and wooden ornaments were also added and a tradition emerged of placing either a star or an angel at the top of the tree.

At the end of the 19th century, electric Christmas lights were produced and have evolved into today's programmable flashing LED systems.

CHRISTMAS DINNER

Although traditions about food at Christmas vary enormously, one common and often central feature is a lavish meal.

Generally called Christmas dinner, it's a time for quality crockery, festive napkins, the best tablecloth and possibly candles.

Christmas dinner traditionally consists of roasted **turkey**, stuffing and gravy, with small sausages wrapped in bacon (often given the enchanting name 'pigs in blankets'). This is served with bread sauce and cranberry sauce, roast potatoes and vegetables – particularly **Brussels sprouts**, carrots and roast parsnips.

If you're following tradition this main course is followed by **Christmas pudding**, or **mince pies** with brandy butter, custard or cream. Pudding or mince pies may be replaced by trifle or a Christmas log. Other customs accompany the meal, such as wearing party hats and pulling **crackers**.

In its idealised form, Christmas dinner involves the entire family, old and young, assembled from far and wide in an unforgettable time of bonding, sharing and caring.

CHRISTMAS EVE

There's an old quote, 'It is better to travel hopefully, than to arrive', attributed to Robert Louis Stevenson. There is something appealing about anticipation when we think about Christmas Eve, the day before **Christmas Day**.

Across most Christian denominations Christmas Eve is a time for services and celebrations. In part, this arises from the idea, present in the Jewish faith, that a day begins at sunset. Some churches ring their **bells** and some hold services on Christmas Eve. Some have a late-night candlelit **carol service** ending just after midnight, which allows participants the experience that they have finally journeyed into Christmas Day. Since tradition holds that Jesus was born at night **(based on Luke 2:8)**, churches celebrate communion on Christmas Eve, often at midnight, in which case it is often called Midnight Mass.

The idea of Jesus being born at night is reflected in some cultures and languages where Christmas Eve is referred to as the 'Holy Night', something echoed in the well-known Christmas carol 'Silent Night, Holy Night'.

As with Christmas celebrations generally, there are enormous variations between different countries and cultures on Christmas Eve. So, for example, in some countries there is a tradition of having a long evening family meal, which takes on the role of the Christmas dinner.

Everywhere there is a sense of anticipation on Christmas Eve, whether it is part of a sacred or secular celebration. Christians can remind themselves of Jesus' humble coming in the past and his anticipated glorious coming again in the future.

CHRISTMAS FILMS

There are many Christmas movie classics. In that category I would include *It's a Wonderful Life*, *A Christmas Carol*, *ELF*, *The Grinch*, *Miracle on 34th Street*, *The Lion, the Witch and the Wardrobe*, *Home Alone* and *Die Hard*.

When you look at Christmas films I think one common theme that emerges is longing.

First, there is a longing for *excitement*. There's a lot of nostalgia in Christmas films, the idea here that as a child, Christmas was enchanting but it loses its charm as we get older. Many Christmas films seek to recreate that lost sense of magic.

Second, there is a longing for *rescue*. Part of the feel-good factor that many Christmas films seek to tap into is the idea of being rescued or, to use an older word, *redeemed*. People feel trapped in jobs, in relationships, in responsibilities for children and parents, or even trapped in life itself. Many Christmas films are about getting out, breaking free, about being released.

Third, there is a longing for *home*. At their heart many Christmas films seem to hold out the ideal of a place beyond our cold, grey and unfriendly world, where there is light, warmth and friendship. They talk of a place we can only refer to as *home*. With that idea of home comes a sense of security; of being able to lock the door against enemies; of being in a place where you can be who you want to be without being threatened by others.

All these longings seem to me to be raising questions that the authentic Christmas answers. The story of God coming to earth in **Christ** is unspeakably thrilling; it is about rescue and redemption from the deepest and darkest of evils, and it tells of a God who wants to bring his people to their eternal home.

Even if few Christmas films give answers worth taking seriously, many raise questions that demand answers.

CHRISTMAS ISLAND

There are a number of Christmas Islands, named, in every case it seems, by captains who discovered them on 25th December.

One Christmas Island is an Australian external territory just south of Indonesia, a mere 135 square kilometres (52 square miles) and with under 2,000 native inhabitants. This has both extraordinary biological importance and, at the time of writing, also holds one of Australia's Immigration Reception and Processing Centres.

Another Christmas Island, now called Kiritimati, is one of the many islands in the Republic of Kiribati in the south-western part of the Pacific Ocean. This Christmas Island is the largest coral atoll in the world with a land area of 388 square kilometres (150 square miles) and a population of 7,000. Formerly a British colony, this Christmas Island is famous for being the site of nuclear bomb tests, including those of hydrogen bombs in the 1950s. Currently it is one of a number of areas that are under threat from sea-level rise caused by global warming.

CHRISTMAS MUSIC

With music's ability to heighten or communicate moods and emotions it's unsurprising that it has long been associated with Christmas.

There's a variety of 'serious' or classical music to do with Christmas. Various composers have created orchestral music that uses festive elements such as carols. Others have composed music based on the idea of sleigh bells; the great favourite is Prokofiev's 'Troika' ('Sleigh Ride') from *Lieutenant Kije*.

With choral music we come to the various oratorios associated with Christmas. An oratorio, it has been claimed with some merit, is simply an opera in which nobody moves. This quality of immobility has had two advantages. The first is that churches, which were unenthusiastic about endorsing opera, found nothing in oratorios to offend them. Victorians loved them. The fact that opera was widely banned during the fasting of the Advent season also boosted ticket sales of oratorios. The second is quite simply that, without either expensive stage sets or the need for singers who can act, oratorios are easier and cheaper to perform.

Two oratorios are commonly performed at Christmas. One is Bach's *Christmas Oratorio*, a compilation of six choral works originally used in church. The great seasonal favourite is, however, George Friedrich Handel's *Messiah*, famed for its '**Hallelujah Chorus**', which definitely merits its own entry.

A number of operas have links with Christmas and Humperdinck's *Hansel and Gretel* is often performed in the Christmas season. With ballets, the most important work is, without doubt, Tchaikovsky's fantasy ballet *The Nutcracker*.

With popular Christmas music, it's difficult to know where to begin. Many of us will have some songs that we love and some we dislike. Bing Crosby's 'White Christmas' of 1942 probably started the genre and many songwriters dream of repeating that enduring success.

CHRISTMAS PUDDING

Christmas pudding seems to be one of those foods you either love or hate. It has its origins from the beginning of Christianity, when porridge was eaten on Christmas Eve to line the stomach after the day's fasting.

Gradually, people added spices, dried fruits and honey to the porridge to make it a special dish for Christmas. Later, in the Middle Ages, it was turned into a pudding called 'frumenty', being so stiff with fruit, they would tie it in a cloth, dunk it into a large cauldron of boiling water and boil it for many hours to make Christmas pudding. In the 17th century, the word 'plum' referred to raisins or other fruits – plum pudding has, in fact, never contained plums.

In Tudor times Christmas pudding was a combination of meat, oatmeal and spices all boiled together. This mixture was then wrapped in pig guts so that the pudding looked like a sausage and could be sliced.

Often, homemade puddings include silver charms and new coins. Whoever finds the charm in their piece of pudding will have good luck in the year to come. This tradition dates right back to ancient Rome and the Saturnalia feast, when it was customary to place a dried bean inside a cake. Whoever found the bean was 'king' for the evening and was able to order other guests to make fools of themselves in a game of dares. This continued until the Victorian Age.

Steamed Christmas pudding is traditionally served with brandy poured over the top, which is then set on fire. It's said that the flaming brandy represents the Passion of **Christ**.

CHRISTMAS TREE

Christmas trees are so associated with Christmas that a simple line drawing of a triangle with zig-zag sides is often enough to indicate the season. Indeed, for many people Christmas begins with the ritual of 'putting up the tree'.

The origin of Christmas trees, like so much else, is shrouded in mystery and subject to competing claims. The fact is that even in the pre-Christian world there were those who, in this darkest part of the year, displayed at least a part of a fir tree in their house. Whatever any pagan associations, this probably reflected the mysterious ability of coniferous fir trees to retain their foliage and appear alive, while deciduous trees lose their leaves and seem dead.

Christians found much that was symbolic in trees. In the Bible there is the tree of the knowledge of good and evil in the Garden of Eden, the 'tree' of the cross at the heart of the gospel, and the return of the tree of paradise in the vision of the new heaven given to John at the end of the Book of Revelation. Various stories contributed to the significance of the fir tree. One relates how Saint Boniface, a missionary to the German people in the 8th century, came across pagans engaged in sacrifice in front of a great oak tree. Boniface simply took an axe to the oak and was then astonished to find a young fir tree sprouting from its roots.

On whatever basis, Christmas trees seem to have become widespread during the Renaissance period, particularly in the area that we now call Germany. Martin Luther welcomed trees as a Christmas symbol and, wherever their faith spread, Christmas trees followed.

In the 19th century the fashion for Christmas trees spread to France and the UK, in the latter case helped by the regal endorsement of Queen Victoria and Prince Albert.

Depictions of the royal tree made it across the Atlantic and Christmas trees became popular in the United States. In the 20th century they spread through every social class. Trees also went from the home into the public space; stores found a decorated Christmas tree to be a good advertisement and soon town halls followed.

Some large public Christmas trees have a history. The classic example is the tree in London's Trafalgar Square, which is a yearly gift from Norway in appreciation for the British support of Norwegian resistance during the Second World War.

As with so much at Christmas time, traditions end up acquiring their own traditions, and so with Christmas trees. It seems to be widely accepted by many people that the tree should be put up on or about the first day of **Advent**, and that they should be taken down by 6th January, **Twelfth Night**.

CRACKERS

Unlike most Christmas traditions, crackers have a clear origin. Tom Smith (1823–1869) was a London sweet-maker and on a visit to Paris was struck by a French habit of wrapping quality sweets in twists of paper. He adopted this and began inserting love messages with his sweets. He was then inspired to add a snap and crackle to his creations, the result being a much larger object. Eventually, he simply dropped the sweet part and the modern cracker was born. Smith's crackers soon became popular and, enhanced by the addition of gifts, paper hats and colourful designs, kept his company in business for nearly a hundred years.

The world's longest cracker measured 63.1 metres (207 feet) long and 4 metres (13 feet) in diameter, and was made by the parents of children at a primary school in Chesham, Buckinghamshire. It was pulled by the children of the school and members of the Saracens Rugby Club on 20th December 2001 . . . and went bang!

Crackers are technically pyrotechnic devices (translated: 'they explode') and it is therefore illegal to sell Christmas crackers to persons younger than twelve years old under *The Pyrotechnic Articles (Safety) Regulations 2015*. You should also be aware that passengers on commercial flights in and to the United States are prohibited from carrying Christmas crackers on board or in checked baggage. The penalties are severe. Don't say I didn't warn you!

CRIB SCENE
(NATIVITY OR MANGER SCENE)

A crib is any basket or frame that can contain a baby's bed and is the normal place for a newborn baby to be placed. In **Luke 2:8-20** a contrast is no doubt intended by the infant Jesus not getting a proper crib but instead a **manger**, an animal feed trough. The word 'crib' is often used in the context of depictions of the first Christmas and a 'crib scene' (or 'nativity' or 'manger' scene) can often mean any sort of physical depiction of the nativity story with baby Jesus, Mary, Joseph, shepherds, wise men and, inevitably, animals.

The earliest Christmas crib was used by Pope Sixtus III around 400. He introduced the idea of Midnight Mass on Christmas Eve in Rome, and built a copy of Jesus' crib in the Church of Santa Maria Maggiore.

The practice of 'visualising' the nativity scene was popularised by St Francis of Assisi in 1223. Wanting to communicate the reality of the birth of **Christ**, in all its poverty and discomfort, to ordinary people, he found a cave near the village of Greccio and placed there a donkey, an ox and a carved figure of a baby lying in a manger. Families from all over the region heard what he had done and visited the site. Another saint, Bonaventure, writing in the 13th century, describes how St Francis came up with the idea:

> That this might not seem an innovation, he sought and obtained licence from the supreme pontiff, and they made ready a manger, and brought hay, together with an ox and an ass, unto the place. The man of God [St Francis] filled with tender love, stood before the manger, bathed in tears, and overflowing with joy. Solemn masses were celebrated over the manger, Francis chanting the Holy Gospel.

Crib scenes grew in popularity, particularly in Catholic countries, and at times, particularly the 18th century, the creation of them was taken very seriously. So, for example, in Naples the finest sculptors and painters were employed to cut and decorate the figures.

In some places live nativity scenes occur, with ordinary people or actors depicting the various individuals in the nativity story. Some, rather boldly, include live animals with the inevitable (and often unintended) entertainment value that live animals always provide.

DICKENS

A 2017 film about Charles Dickens was entitled *The Man Who Invented Christmas*. The eye-catching title is a profound exaggeration because, as this book frequently points out, there is much about Christmas festivities that goes very much further back than the Victorian period.

It's hard to argue with the majority view that Dickens was the greatest novelist of the Victorian period, not least in the number of memorable books and characters that he created.

Born in Portsmouth in 1812, Dickens had a long encounter with poverty in early adolescence, which fuelled an anger about social injustice that runs through much of his works.

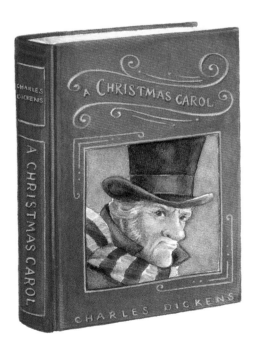

Dickens wrote numerous novels, often in instalments, with his pioneering cliff-hanger endings creating a growing readership that longed to know what was going to happen. He had a gift for humour, satire and social comment, and delighted in creating characters, some of them grotesque, who his readers either loved or hated.

He toured the United States and in doing so became one of the first authors to be popular on both sides of the Atlantic. Increasingly a public figure he undertook numerous tours, during which he read his works to large audiences. He died suddenly in 1870 at the age of 58.

Dickens wrote a number of Christmas stories, the most famous of which, *A Christmas Carol*, was published in 1843. He took the idea of a ghost story and turned it into a moral tale of judgement and salvation at Christmas.

At the time of the publication of *A Christmas Carol* the Christmas season was not greatly celebrated. Dickens, reaching back to an imagined past, delivered a vision of a perfect Christmas, full of **turkey**, **mistletoe**, **snow** on the ground, **carol** singers on the street and, amid the distant sound of church **bells**, cheerful families gathered around tables overflowing with food and goodwill. It was an enticing portrayal – sometimes called the Victorian Christmas – that caught on and even a century and a half later it is still possible to recognise Dickens' vision in the popular portrayal of Christmas in Britain and elsewhere.

ELIZABETH AND ZECHARIAH

Luke begins his account of the nativity of Jesus in what might seem a rather surprising way. We are introduced to Zechariah, a priest in the temple at Jerusalem at the time of **Herod the Great**, and his wife Elizabeth, whose name means 'My God has sworn an oath'. Against every expectation they become parents as Elizabeth gives birth to John, who will subsequently bear the title of the Baptist, a man who plays a very significant role in preparing the way for the ministry of Jesus.

Luke takes care to mention what might be called 'the qualifications' of both Zechariah and Elizabeth. Both are from priestly families that go back to Aaron, a man who was prophet, priest and brother of Moses, and both are 'righteous in the sight of God, observing all the Lord's commands and decrees blamelessly' **(Luke 1:6)**. They are, however, childless – we are told that 'Elizabeth could not conceive' – and are both very old. In this sort of culture, childlessness is a source of shame because it not only brings the risk of unsupported poverty in old age but marks the end of the all-important family line. Sadly, the burden of this shame inevitably falls on the woman and, indeed, Elizabeth refers to her childlessness as 'her disgrace' in **Luke 1:25**. Nevertheless, despite their age, the couple continue to pray for a child.

As Zechariah is performing his appointed duty as a priest in the temple in Jerusalem, an **angel** – Gabriel – appears and says his prayers have been heard and that Elizabeth will bear a son who will 'make ready a people prepared for the Lord' (Luke 1:17). Zechariah expresses some scepticism about this and as a result Gabriel takes away his power of speech. The mute Zechariah returns home and Elizabeth becomes pregnant, remaining in seclusion for five months.

Elizabeth now plays a significant role in relation to Mary, to whom she is related (tradition says that they were cousins, but the Greek simply means a 'relative'). In Nazareth, Mary is told of Elizabeth's pregnancy possibly as an encouragement that, after centuries of silence, God is now once more acting in power for his people. Mary heads southwards to Judea to visit Elizabeth and at their encounter we read that the baby leapt in Elizabeth's womb and she was 'filled with the Holy Spirit'. In Luke's two-volume work – the Gospel of Luke and the Acts of the Apostles – Elizabeth is the first individual to be 'filled with the Holy Spirit'. Empowered by the Spirit, Elizabeth blesses Mary and the child and says, 'But why am I so favoured, that the mother of my Lord should come to me? As soon as the sound of your greeting reached my ears, the baby in my womb leaped for joy' (Luke 1:43-44).

Mary stays with Elizabeth for three months before returning to Nazareth. The focus of the gospel now shifts back to Elizabeth's own pregnancy as amid great joy and celebration amongst family and friends she gives birth to a son. Zechariah is still silent but when the decision is taken, in accordance with tradition, to name the child after his father, Elizabeth boldly intervenes saying that 'he is to be called John'.

This is confirmed when Zechariah spells out on a writing tablet that the child's name is indeed going to be John. With this Elizabeth disappears from the Bible record.

Although her role is easily overlooked, Elizabeth is both a sign and encouragement. She is a sign of one of the great themes of the gospel, that God will, and does, operate and act through the little people, the marginalised and even those who feel they are shamed. A woman who felt she was disgraced becomes filled with the Holy Spirit and, prompted by the son in her womb, becomes a prophet, the first person to give Jesus that very highest of titles 'the Lord'.

Elizabeth is also a profound encouragement. In her unfortunate situation she prays and is indeed blessed with an answer. Like other 'barren women' in the Bible (Sarah, Genesis 18:11; Rebekah, Genesis 25:21; Rachel, Genesis 29:31; Samson's mother, Judges 13:2-3; and Hannah, 1 Samuel 1 – 2) God does in fact let her become the mother of a very special child. Although for many couples today childlessness remains a great sorrow, God can still respond in either granting conception or a contented acceptance of the situation.

The word that we translate as 'gospel' literally means 'good news' and Elizabeth lives it out. In the story of Elizabeth we don't just see the start of the gospel, we see exactly what it's all about: despair ended, hope restored and the insignificant becoming truly significant.

EPIPHANY

Epiphany is a Christian feast that celebrates the visit of the **wise men** or **Magi** to the infant Jesus. The word 'epiphany' comes from the Greek '*epipháneia*' where it means 'an appearance' or 'a manifestation'. It's important to note that the 'appearance' is not that of the wise men appearing bringing gifts to honour Jesus, but that God in his mercy is allowing Jesus to appear to the Gentiles, those outside the Jewish people. It is as if the giving that is celebrated here is not *from* the wise men and the peoples they represent, but *to* them.

For the Western churches Epiphany falls on 6th January, the famous 'twelfth day' of Christmas. For the Eastern churches, which still follow the Julian calendar, the thirteen-day difference between their calendar and our Gregorian one means it is celebrated on what for us is 19th January. Certainly, in Western churches the significance of Epiphany is that it brings the Christmas season to an end.

FLIGHT TO EGYPT

In our time, the phrase the 'Flight to Egypt' sounds as if it is describing a trip to Cairo, but better termed the 'Escape to Egypt', it is a brief but significant story in Matthew's gospel which closes the account of **Christ's** nativity.

We read that after the **wise men** left,

An angel of the Lord appeared to Joseph in a dream. 'Get up,' he said, 'take the child and his mother and escape to Egypt. Stay there until I tell you, for Herod is going to search for the child to kill him.' So he got up, took the child and his mother during the night and left for Egypt, where he stayed until the death of Herod. And so was fulfilled what the Lord had said through the prophet: 'Out of Egypt I called my son.' (Matthew 2:13-15)

The prophecy referred to is **Hosea 11:1**.

After the account of what is traditionally known as the 'Massacre of the Innocents', the story of Jesus and his family continues.

After Herod died, an angel of the Lord appeared in a dream to Joseph in Egypt and said, 'Get up, take the child and his mother and go to the land of Israel, for those who were trying to take the child's life are dead.' So he got up, took the child and his mother and went to the land of Israel. (Matthew 2:19-21)

In one sense this is simply an escape story. Despite the pious words of Herod to the wise men about wanting to worship the infant 'King of the Jews', the paranoid king had in fact decided to ruthlessly eliminate any threat to his throne in typical Herodian fashion. **Joseph** – the head of the family – is told in a dream to take action and, not even waiting till dawn, takes the child (Jesus is no longer described as a baby) and Mary and leaves for Egypt, a place with a very large Jewish community, well outside the authority of **Herod the Great**.

You could see this as the infant Jesus experiencing the plight of so many in our world in being forced to flee from persecution and become a refugee. This is, doubtless, valid but there is more here. In the history of the Jewish people, the most important event was their stay of several hundred years in Egypt from which they were rescued by God in the Exodus. One of the themes of the New Testament is the way in which Jesus identifies with God's people, to the point where, in effect, he stands in their place.

GOODWILL

Christmas has its seasonal clichés and one of them is that it is 'a season of goodwill'.

'Goodwill' means to 'will good' to others. It is to wish others well; to have friendly, helpful, or cooperative feelings or attitudes towards them. But why is it linked *specifically* with Christmas? The link with Christmas goes back to the Authorised Version's translation of the **angel's** message to the **shepherds** in Luke 2:14 which reads:

> Glory to God in the highest, and on earth peace, good will toward men.

With modern versions we get: 'on earth peace to those on whom his favour rests' (NIV) or 'peace on earth to those with whom God is pleased' (NLT).

The great Bible message of **Christ's** coming is the good news of God's grace, charity and kindness extended out to the entire human race, and good news to the human race should spill over into our goodwill to others.

HALLELUJAH CHORUS

George Friederich Handel's *Messiah* is probably the most popular piece of all classical **Christmas music**. Technically an oratorio (an 'opera without action'), it focuses more on Easter than Christmas but, nevertheless, performances of *Messiah* are almost universal in the run-up to Christmas.

Handel (1685–1759) was a German musician who settled in London and became a part of the British musical scene with a prolific output of operas, oratorios and various other works. He was a Christian and a generous supporter of good causes.

In summer 1741 Handel was sent the text of *Messiah* by the wealthy landowner and devout Anglican Charles Jennens, who had supported Handel financially in the past. Jennens' text doesn't so much tell the story of Jesus as compile a series of biblical texts that refer to his coming as **Messiah**, his death on the cross, his resurrection and ultimate triumph. Handel, who had the ability to write music fast, began working on it at what was, even for him, an extraordinary pace. Within twenty-four days he had written fifty-three movements of choral and orchestral music, totalling some two hours.

In spring 1742 Handel conducted the first performance of *Messiah* in Dublin for a charity concert. Handel's reputation was such that it was a sell out and, to maximise numbers, men were requested to avoid bringing swords and women to avoid wearing hoops in their dresses. The work was an immediate success in Dublin but less so when performed in London, where there were pious suspicions that the playhouse was inappropriate for religious music.

With repeated performances, many of them for such charities as London's Foundling Hospital, *Messiah* won the hearts of music lovers and soon became a tradition. In the 18th and 19th centuries the practice grew up of performing it with the largest and loudest forces, with massed choirs and enormous orchestras.

The most well-known movement of this work is the remarkable 'Hallelujah Chorus', which concludes the second of the three parts. It is said that on first hearing it King George II, possibly imagining that he was hearing the national anthem of heaven, rose to his feet, compelling the rest of the audience also to stand. The tradition persists.

Messiah is an astonishing work and deserves to be listened to thoughtfully, not just at Christmas but at any time of the year.

HANUKKAH

Although the events that Hanukkah commemorates are well known to those of the Jewish faith, they remain almost unknown by others for the simple reason that they fall into 'the gap' between our Old and New Testaments. So here's a summary of the events behind Hanukkah.

Around 300 BC the Near East was conquered by the Greek-speaking Seleucid Empire who were to govern much of the area for approximately 250 years. Within that empire, one particularly malevolent king was Antiochus Epiphanes (215–164 BC). Antiochus developed a hatred of the Jewish people that he governed and unleashed a barbaric onslaught upon them.

The focus of his anger fell on the heart of the Jewish faith – the temple in Jerusalem. Antiochus sacrificed pigs on the altar, banned sacrifices and brutally executed anybody who protested. In 165 BC the result of these outrages was an uprising – the Maccabean Revolt – in which the Jews regained power over Jerusalem, and the temple was cleansed and rededicated.

Hanukkah, the Festival of Dedication, arose as a commemoration of the cleansing of the temple. It became associated with many rituals and traditions, often focusing on light, and is sometimes referred to as the 'Festival of Lights'. It occurs in the New Testament where we read in **John 10:22-23**, 'Then came the Festival of Dedication at Jerusalem. It was winter, and Jesus was in the temple courts walking in Solomon's Colonnade.'

Today Hanukkah is widely celebrated in the Jewish community. It often involves the public display of a special *menorah*, a candelabra with nine lamps instead of the usual seven, and a series of rituals performed every day throughout an eight-day holiday. There are special additions to the daily prayer service and blessings after meals.

The 1st-century Jewish historian Josephus claimed that Hanukkah marked a victory of light over darkness. As a believer in Jesus as the Messiah, I see the fulfilment of that hope in **John 1:4-5** where we read that in Jesus 'was life, and that life was the light of all mankind. The light shines in the darkness, and the darkness has not overcome it'.

HEROD THE GREAT

Herod was appointed by the Roman Senate to be King of Judea in 40 BC, and by 37 BC he controlled most of current-day Israel and Palestine. He even called himself 'King of the Jews' and was known by that title until his death. That's why he was threatened when he heard that someone had been born who was being called King of the Jews.

Herod was ruthless and his palace was full of intrigue and tragedy. His paranoia was legendary. He executed his uncle, his mother-in-law, his wife Mariamme, two of his sons and a barber. His entire life was one of plotting and execution. After the birth of Jesus he ordered the slaughter of all the boys under the age of two in **Bethlehem**, in an attempt to kill Jesus, the 'baby King'. This is known as the 'Slaughter of the Innocents' and is recorded in Matthew's gospel. In medieval times, this event was remembered as 'Childermass' and celebrated on 28th December. Today it is more commonly referred to as Holy Innocent's Day.

Josephus, a Jewish historian, wrote a few years after Herod's death:

> He was no king but the most cruel tyrant who ever ascended the throne. He murdered a vast number of people and the lot of those he left was so miserable that the dead might count themselves fortunate . . . within a few years the Jews suffered more misery through Herod than their forefathers had done.

Herod was replaced by his son Herod Antipas (21 BC – AD 39), who ruled throughout the ministry of Jesus.

IMMANUEL

Sometimes a single word can contain a lot of truth and this is certainly the case with 'Immanuel' or, as it was written in older Bibles, 'Emmanuel'. The word occurs just once in the pages of the New Testament but the idea behind it runs through the whole Bible. Conveniently rhyming with 'dwell', '**Noël**' and 'Israel', Immanuel turns up frequently in Christmas hymns and **carols** as in 'Pleased as man with man to dwell; Jesus, our Emmanuel' from 'Hark! The Herald Angels Sing'.

In the first chapter of Matthew's gospel we read how **Joseph** is told by an **angel** in a dream that Mary is going to conceive through the Holy Spirit and will give birth to a son, who he is to call Jesus. Matthew then tells us:

> **All this took place to fulfil what the Lord had said through the prophet: 'The virgin will conceive and give birth to a son, and they will call him Immanuel' (which means 'God with us').** (Matthew 1:22-23)

As with so much in the nativity accounts there's a rich background here. First of all there's a direct reference to prophetic verses in Isaiah, which refer to a child who will be called 'God with us' (Isaiah 7:14, 8:8, 8:10). The most important of these is **7:14**, which Matthew quotes and refers to a virgin conceiving. In the angel's message to Joseph, Matthew sees the fulfilling of this prophecy: the miraculous birth of a child who, in some way, will be 'God with us'. This anticipation of a glorious, divine individual fits well with the fact that Isaiah is full of many references to a coming **Messiah**, who will be both God's servant and King and save his people.

The second thing is that the very idea of the presence of God with his people is one of the 'master themes' of the Bible. In Genesis we read that 'in the beginning' human beings knew the presence of God and had fellowship with him. Their tragic rebellion against God resulted in an appalling break in relations between humankind and God, something that has continued ever since. Deep down, we are all naturally those who have chosen to keep God at a distance.

The story of the Old Testament is of God, acting over centuries in love mixed with discipline, bringing people back to himself. It's there in the giving of the old covenant with its promises by God and the obligation of obedience that it expects in response. It's there in the messages of the prophets and, above all, in the creation of the temple where, at its very core, God was in some way present with his people. Yet the temple system was very limited in granting any access to God. Only one man, the high priest, and he only on one day a year, could venture beyond the great curtain and enter the 'holy of holies' and stand before God.

By quoting this passage about 'God with us' Matthew is saying that something astonishingly new is happening: through this infant we will be able to meet with God. That theme of Jesus giving access to God is picked up elsewhere in Matthew's gospel. So we read that when Jesus died on the cross, 'at that moment the curtain of the temple was torn in two from top to bottom' (Matthew 27:51). This theme of Immanuel – God with us – continues to the very last verse of Matthew's gospel where the resurrected Jesus declares to his followers, 'And surely I am with you always, to the very end of the age' (Matthew 28:20). The promise of God now being with his people through Jesus and the Holy Spirit weaves its way in and out of the letters of the New Testament and culminates in the glorious vision of God dwelling eternally with his people at the end of the Book of Revelation.

If we understand this, we can see what a tremendous comfort this idea is. We can have access to God. In **Christ**, God has come close to us. Those who come to Jesus and accept him as their Saviour have the privilege of knowing God as a loving parent. In the difficulties and challenges of life, this presence of God is deeply encouraging. In Jesus, God stands alongside us in the hospital, when we sit alone at home, when we face temptation and when the darkness of death looms before us. The tremendous news of Christmas is that those who come to Jesus no longer need to be alone. In Jesus, 'God is with us.'

INCARNATION

In the incarnation we plunge deep to the very heart of Christmas. The word 'incarnation' comes from the Latin '*in carne*' – 'in the flesh'. It refers to God appearing bodily, in a way that it is impossible to fully understand and define, the baby in the **Bethlehem** manger was not just human but also God. A belief in the incarnation – referred to as the 'deity of **Christ**' – is central to all traditional Christianity and is present in every creed or statement of faith of all authentically Christian denominations.

The incarnation is also a belief that is widely expressed in Christmas **carols** and hymns. Take, for instance, 'Hark! The Herald Angels Sing' with 'Veiled in flesh the Godhead see, Hail the incarnate Deity'. Or 'O Come, All Ye Faithful', which has the lines:

God of God, Light of Light,
Lo! he abhors not the Virgin's womb;
Very God, begotten, not created.

In fact, given the way that the word 'Lord' is used throughout the Bible mainly as a term for God, any reference to the 'Lord Jesus' in the context of Christmas – or anywhere else – is to acknowledge his status as God. Even 'Away in a Manger' comes up with the awesome claim, 'Little Lord Jesus'.

At Christmas, and other times of the year, the question is often asked: why was it necessary for God to become one of us in Jesus? Let me offer two answers.

The first answer is that the incarnation shows God's involvement and commitment to the human race. We are not left alone. God has identified with us and knows about human existence from, as it were, his personal experience. When we struggle in pain it's often tempting to say to God, 'You don't know what I'm suffering!' Yet with the incarnation God can, as it were, show us his pierced hands and say, 'Oh, but I do.'

The second and far deeper answer takes us to the cross and something that every gospel writer highlights: Jesus acting there in some way as a representative of the human race. For him to do that, it was not enough for him to claim to be human; he had indeed to be authentically human. One common view of the cross is that there, Jesus bore the punishment that was rightfully ours and, by doing so, paid off all our 'debts' to God and so set us free. As a human being, Jesus had the right to do this; and as God, he had the infinite power to achieve it. In one sense that takes us beyond Christmas; on the other hand the birth of Jesus and his cradling in the humility of a wooden manger points to his death on a wooden cross. The incarnation allows God to be alongside us; it also allows God to be for us.

JOSEPH

Joseph is a key figure in the nativity story. He was a devout man from Nazareth, from the 'house and line of David' (**Luke 2:4**) and he was a carpenter (**Matthew 13:55**), although the Greek word used could mean 'a builder' or 'a craftsman'. That Joseph was a good man is demonstrated when, faced with what seems to be evidence of fornication by Mary to whom he is engaged, he chooses to divorce her privately to avoid public scandal (**Matthew 1:19**). However, an **angel** of the Lord appears to Joseph in a dream and reveals that the child that Mary will bear is conceived by the Holy Spirit and that Joseph is to give him the name Jesus (**Matthew 1:18-22**). (That Joseph does indeed give the child the name Jesus means he has taken him to be his own child; in effect he adopts Jesus.) Acting on the dream, Joseph takes Mary as his wife, although the text is explicit that she remains a virgin until after Jesus is born.

Compelled by a census, which may well have involved inherited land ownership, Joseph returns to his ancestral home **Bethlehem**, taking Mary with him (**Luke 2:1-5**). There he finds basic accommodation where the baby is born.

In the nativity story, Joseph next appears with Mary taking the infant Jesus to present him to the Lord at the temple in Jerusalem; an event where they meet Simeon and Anna (Luke 2:22-38).

Then, after the visit of the **wise men**, quite possibly months later, Joseph again has another dream encounter with an angel, in which he is told to get up, take the child and his mother and escape to Egypt because **Herod** wants to kill the baby. Joseph obeys immediately (Matthew 2:13-15).

After an unspecified time in Egypt, Joseph has another visitation of an angel in a dream and is told it is time to return to Israel because the threat against the child has been lifted (Matthew 2:19-23). He goes to Judea but, wary of Herod's son who has taken power, and being warned in another dream (Matthew 2:22), he takes the family back to Nazareth in Galilee.

Outside the accounts of the nativity we have just one more mention of an action of Joseph and that is Jesus' trip to Jerusalem when he is twelve (Luke 2:41-50). Although Joseph seems to have passed on his trade of carpenter or craftsman to Jesus (Mark 6:3), he doesn't appear during the ministry of Jesus, which leads many people to assume that he had probably died before then. This may allow us to infer that he was actually much older than Mary, something perfectly common in that culture.

Joseph is only very briefly and incidentally in the limelight in the nativity story, yet he plays the supporting role that he is called to faithfully: he leads, protects and provides. When he has to act, he acts decisively, faithfully and quickly. Supporting roles may not be appealing but they are essential. If that's what we are called to, may we do it faithfully.

KING WENCESLAS

Wenceslas, born in 907 in the castle of Stochov, near Prague, was not actually a king but Duke of Bohemia. The castle no longer stands but there is still an oak tree that was supposedly planted by Ludmila, his Christian grandmother, when Wenceslas was born.

At first Ludmila raised him. Then, when he was about thirteen years old, his father died and Wenceslas succeeded him as duke. Because he was too young to rule, his mother, Drahomira, became regent. Drahomira was opposed to Christianity and used her new power to persecute followers of the Christian faith. She refused to let Wenceslas see Ludmila because she was afraid they would scheme to overthrow her. Eventually, Ludmila was murdered at Tetin Castle – strangled, it is said, at Drahomira's command. After her death Ludmila was revered as a saint.

The loss of his grandmother did not stop Wenceslas from seizing power. At the age of eighteen he overthrew his mother's regency, just as she had feared, and began to rule for himself.

A stern but fair monarch, he stopped the persecution of priests and tamed the rebellious nobility. He was known for his kindness to the poor, as depicted in later verses of the **carol**. He was especially charitable to children, helping young orphans and slaves.

Many of the Bohemian nobles resented Wenceslas' attempts to spread Christianity, and were displeased when he swore allegiance to the king of Germany, Henry I. The duke's most deadly enemy proved to be his own brother, Boleslav, who joined the nobles in plotting his brother's assassination. He invited Wenceslas to a religious festival and then attacked him on his way to Mass. As the two were struggling, Boleslav's supporters jumped in and murdered Wenceslas. He was in his early twenties and had ruled Bohemia for five years.

The Holy Roman Emperor Otto the Great bestowed the title King on Wenceslas posthumously, and today he is remembered as the patron saint of the Czech Republic. We associate Wenceslas with 26th December because, as the carol tells us, it was 'on the feast of Stephen' that the good king went gathering fuel for his poorer subjects. Actually, St Wenceslas Day is 28th December, for the king was killed on that day in 929.

The words to the carol 'Good King Wenceslas' were written by John Mason Neale and first published in 1853. It is an unusual carol because it has no reference to the nativity. Yet it conveys the 'Christmas spirit' and encourages generosity to the poor, as in the last few lines:

Therefore, Christian men, be sure
Wealth or rank possessing,
Ye who now will bless the poor
Shall yourselves find blessing.

LIGHT AND LIGHTS

Light is a recurrent motif at this time of year. Of course, in the Northern Hemisphere this is a theme that comes supported by inescapable visual imagery: the gap between dawn and dusk in December can seem dreadfully short. In fact, many of us go to work in darkness, work in artificial light and return home when night has already fallen.

It's virtually certain that, however far back you trace festivities at this time of the year, one of the central elements was the bringing of light through either fires or candles. Whether with Christmas tree lights, festive illuminations or in candlelit services, there is something heart-warming and, in the best sense, *magical* about lights at Christmas.

Light is an image that flows throughout the Bible, quite literally from the first to the last page. At the very beginning of the Bible we read:

> And God said, 'Let there be light,' and there was light. God saw that the light was good, and he separated the light from the darkness. (Genesis 1:3-4)

At the very end of the Bible we read of God's people in the new creation:

> There will be no more night. They will not need the light of a lamp or the light of the sun, for the Lord God will give them light. (Revelation 22:5)

Lights were prominent in the temple with the idea that, at the very heart of the temple, God was present in glorious light. It is no accident that the symbol of the Jewish faith is the sacred candelabra, the *menorah*.

God is seen as light and the images of the coming **Messiah** are often linked with light. Consider the Christmas verse of Isaiah 9:2:

> The people walking in darkness have seen a great light; on those living in the land of deep darkness a light has dawned.

In **Matthew 4:15-16** this verse is applied to Jesus himself.

Simeon calls **Christ** 'a light for revelation to the Gentiles, and the glory of your people Israel' (**Luke 2:32**). It is in John's gospel that the image of light is most firmly linked with Christ, with repeated references to Jesus as light in the opening verses (**John 1:4, 5, 7, 8, 9**). Later in that gospel Jesus himself declares that he is 'the light of the world' (**John 8:12**) and claims:

> I have come into the world as a light, so that no one who believes in me should stay in darkness. (**John 12:46**)

THE LION, THE WITCH AND THE WARDROBE

On the surface, C.S. Lewis' classic of fantasy *The Lion, the Witch and the Wardrobe* is only marginally about Christmas. Yet at a deeper level, the theme of Christmas runs all the way through it. It's not surprising, then, that the story appears at Christmas, whether on screen or on stage.

The Lion, the Witch and the Wardrobe was the first of seven children's novels written by Lewis, and is set in the fantasy world of Narnia, governed by the great lion Aslan who is an image of **Christ**. It was written in the late 1940s at a time when Lewis was already a distinguished Oxford academic and a prolific writer on Christian topics.

One Christmas link in *The Lion, the Witch and the Wardrobe* is that Narnia has fallen under the spell of the White Witch, with the result that, in a famous phrase, it 'is always winter but never Christmas'.

Another seasonal link comes with the appearance of **Father Christmas** bearing gifts and, with him, the beginning of the end of winter's long, cruel reign.

Whether at Christmas or at any other time, *The Lion, the Witch and the Wardrobe* and the other six Narnia books are well worth a read.

MAGNIFICAT

The Magnificat refers to the joyful song of Mary at the **Annunciation** that we find in **Luke 1:46-55**, which is used in church services and not only at Christmas. The name 'the Magnificat' comes from the Latin '*Magnificat anima mea Dominum*' or 'my soul magnifies the Lord'.

The Magnificat draws on the language of the Old Testament, suggesting that Mary knew the scriptures well. In her song, Mary humbly rejoices in the privilege granted her of bearing the **Messiah**. She glorifies God as she looks forward to how, through her son, the world will be changed by the bringing down of the powerful, the lifting up of the humble, and the feeding of the hungry. Mary ends by praising God that in the Messiah he has fulfilled his ancient promise to Abraham.

MANGER

The word 'manger' is one that most of us only use at Christmas time. A manger is a long trough for feeding horses or cattle, something that is essential if you're going to have animals stabled close together; you can't just throw the food on the floor of a stable.

Normally a baby would be put in a cradle, but to be forced to use a manger instead of a cradle is a sign of poverty and humility.

The fact that there is something distinctively remarkable about a baby in a manger is clearly implied in the **angel's** instruction to the **shepherds** (**Luke 2:11**) that a sign of the Saviour, 'the Messiah, the Lord' having been born, is the fact that he is a baby wrapped in cloths and lying in a manger.

MERRY
AND MERRIMENT

Christmas is traditionally considered to be the time in which we are 'merry'. In fact, one Christmas greeting that is so common that we have ceased to think about it is 'Merry Christmas!' and we sing 'We wish you a Merry Christmas' without a second thought. Strictly speaking, all 'merry' means is 'cheerful and lively'.

That idea of merriment is present in the **carol** below:

God rest ye merry, gentlemen
Let nothing you dismay,
For Jesus Christ our Saviour, was born upon this Day.
To save us all from Satan's power
When we were gone astray:
O tidings of comfort and joy, comfort and joy,
O tidings of comfort and joy.

What the carol is saying here could perhaps be phrased as 'put your temporary concerns to one side because we have a Saviour who has delivered us from all evil in this world and the next'.

To me that's not just the best basis for merriment; it's the only real basis.

MESSIAH

'Messiah' is the rendering of the Hebrew word '*massiah*' and as such occurs in the Old Testament and is used amongst Jews to this day to refer to the idea of a saviour king who will come to deliver his people. '**Christ**' comes from the Greek word '*Christos*', which is how the early translators of the Old Testament into Greek translated '*massiah*'. Both '*massiah*' and '*Christos*' carry the idea of anointing with oil: something that marks the prophets, priests and kings of the Old Testament.

Having said that, there is in fact a subtle and important difference between the two words. Jews in the Old Testament looked forward, and still look forward, to the Messiah with anticipation as a figure who is to come. Christians, in contrast, have a different perspective: they look back on the Christ as the one who has delivered his people from sin while, at the same time, anticipating his final complete and utter rule after his second coming.

MINCE PIES

The origin of the word 'mince' comes from the Latin '*minutia*', meaning 'smallness'; and 'pie' from the Latin '*pica*', meaning 'magpie'. Used because the various combinations of pie ingredients are compared to objects randomly collected by a magpie.

The origins of mince pies can be traced far back into history. Twelfth-century European knights, returning from

Crusades in the Holy Land, brought back with them many Middle Eastern ways of cooking. Recipes of meat cooked with fruit and sweet spices were popular then, mixing sweet tastes with savoury.

In Tudor times mince pies were still a mixture of meat and fruit. They were called 'shrid' pies because they were made by shredding the meat and suet. Dried fruit would be added, along with cinnamon, cloves and nutmeg. These three spices were said to be symbolic of the three gifts given by the **wise men** to Jesus. The mixture was placed in an oblong tin and, being representative of Jesus' **crib**, a small figure made of pastry often decorated the lid. These pies were much larger than the mince pies we are used to today.

One pie in 1770 is recorded as having among its ingredients: a hare, a pheasant, a capon, two rabbits, two pigeons, two partridges, as well as eggs, pickled mushrooms and spices. Sometimes these 'crib' pies would weigh as much as 220 pounds (99.8 kilogrammes).

Jack Horner was steward to the Abbot of Glastonbury, and he had to take a pie to King Henry VII as a gift from the abbot. Under the crust were the title deeds of twelve manor houses, sent to the king in the hope that he would not destroy Glastonbury Abbey. It is said that King Henry received only eleven deeds. What happened to the missing deed? That remains a mystery but a song has been written remembering Jack:

Little Jack Horner,
Sat in the corner,
Eating his Christmas pie.
He stuck in his thumb,
And pulled out a plum,
And said, 'What a good boy am I!'

As with many other Christmas traditions, Oliver Cromwell and the puritans tried to ban mince pies. The ban was lifted when Charles II reinstated Christmas. During the 19th century the mince pie underwent a major change. The new pie was round instead of the traditional oblong, and the meat was replaced with **nuts**, apples and raisins. The pie was therefore much sweeter and instead of being offered at the beginning of a meal was saved for the finale.

MISTLETOE

Mistletoe, widely used as a Christmas decoration, is particularly obvious in winter when its dense bush of dark green leaves and white berries stand out from the bare branches of the host tree, which supplies it with water and nutrients.

Mistletoe is associated with all sorts of ancient beliefs, often linked with fertility – it is, after all, one of the few plants visibly alive in midwinter. The Romans saw mistletoe as an emblem of peace, love and understanding but also hung sprigs of it over doorways as protection against evil.

When Christianity took over Western culture, traditions associated with mistletoe continued.

Mistletoe increasingly became associated with Christmas. Its use as a defence against evil supernatural forces seems to have lingered and may underlie the way in which it is often mounted over doorways. More importantly, perhaps due to its ancient association with fertility, mistletoe became associated with romance, with kissing under the mistletoe recorded as early as the 18th century amongst servants.

MULLED WINE

Mulled or spiced wine is an alcoholic drink usually made with red wine along with various spices, and is served hot or warm. It is a traditional drink during winter, especially around Christmas, and in various forms is often served at seasonal markets across Europe.

Mulled wine seems to go back to Roman times where it probably provided a much-needed antidote to the chills of northern Europe for soldiers and others more used to a Mediterranean climate. By the Middle Ages, mulled wine had acquired a medicinal role. In fact, given the sterilising nature of both alcohol and heat, mulled wine may have indeed been healthier than any local water.

There are various recipes for mulled wine but key ingredients include some or all of the following: orange, lemon, cinnamon, nutmeg, fennel seed, cloves, cardamom and ginger.

NOËL

Noël came into English from French, where '*la fête de Noël*' remains the commonest phrase for the Christmas season and ultimately originates in the Latin words '*nasci*', meaning 'be born', and '*natalis*', meaning 'birthday'.

Noël in English goes back to at least the 12th century and probably came over from the Continent with William the Conqueror in 1066. It makes an appearance in numerous **carols**, the most popular being 'The First Noël' where you can sing the word twenty-nine times.

NUTS

Nuts turn up in many ways at Christmas. They can be given as presents, placed in bowls to nibble or used in cooking either as whole nuts, fractured (as in nougat) or ground up as a paste (as in marzipan).

One of the main characteristics of nuts is that they are a food that can be stored and, in the Northern Hemisphere when there is little fresh food available in winter, they have long been part of a winter diet.

Although nuts have traditionally been part of the Christmas diet, and even been used as festive ornaments, they, like so much associated with the season, have become much more diverse over time. Whereas once Christmas nuts would have been only hazelnuts, walnuts and almonds, it's now common to find peanuts, Brazil nuts, cashews, pistachios, macadamias, pine nuts and chestnuts.

With the rise of vegetarianism, nuts have also become more common as a major element in Christmas meals, although the reality of so many people with nut allergies means that warnings need to be given and alternatives offered.

It seems clear that, in the past at least, nuts had a symbolic importance. With the spread of Christianity across Europe the symbolism changed. So there were ingenious attempts to make the hazelnut represent the Trinity through the fact that it has a shell, a skin and a kernel.

A more interesting thought can be found in the writings of the 14th-century mystic, Lady Julian of Norwich, who had a vision in which she saw a small object like a hazelnut in her palm. When she asked what it was, she was told, 'It is all that is made.' It's an interesting image of the greatness of God compared to his creation and something to think about in the context of the **incarnation**.

The nutcracker, of course, plays an important part in Tchaikovsky's ballet of the same name, which, set at Christmas, is very much a seasonal favourite.

Finally, should conversation flag as you crack the walnuts and break open the almonds, let me offer you a proverb for consideration: 'God gives us nuts, but we have to break them ourselves.'

PEACE

Peace is certainly one of the seasonal values. One of the great prophetic passages in Isaiah talks about the **Messiah** as being someone who can be called 'Wonderful Counsellor, Mighty God, Everlasting Father, Prince of Peace' **(Isaiah 9:6)**. Jesus is the one known as the 'Prince of Peace'. That role of **Christ** is echoed in the **angel's** message to the **shepherds**, 'Glory to God in highest heaven, and peace on earth to those with whom God is pleased' **(Luke 2:13–14 NLT)**.

Two thousand years on from the first Christmas and we still look for peace. In 1971 John Lennon wrote a song entitled 'Happy Xmas (War Is Over)'. Ever since the reaction has been, 'Sorry, John, it isn't.'

First, what does peace mean? Here we are helped by the great emphasis on peace in the Old Testament, with the result that one of the few Hebrew words that many people know is *shalom*. It is something far richer than a mere ceasefire and includes such ideas as fulfilment, justice and happiness. In situations where there have been grievances or damage, *shalom* encourages restoration and of making whole anything that has been broken. The idea of *shalom*, with its proactive ideas of doing something to bring about peace and end hostility, is carried forward into the New Testament and should be part of any Christian thinking about peace. So, in other words, we are not just to enjoy peace but to help *make* peace. Indeed, as Jesus himself says, 'Blessed are the peacemakers, for they will be called children of God' **(Matthew 5:9)**.

Second, we need to recognise that there are different dimensions where peace is needed. There are three different areas that are hungry for peace: *vertical peace* between humanity and God; *lateral peace* between individuals, societies and nations; and *internal peace* within ourselves. At the heart of so many of the world's problems, and perhaps deep down all of them, is the sad fact that every human being has rebelled against God and needs to be reconciled back to him. The coming of **Christ** and, in particular, his bearing of the burden of human sin on the cross at Easter, has broken down the barriers between us and God. The price we couldn't pay for our own forgiveness has been completely paid by him. If we as individuals have that personal experience of being forgiven it helps us greatly when we have to deal with other conflicts. We know something of both the value and cost of forgiveness.

It is easy to despair of peace; to think that human conflict is just one of the things that is inevitable and that there is nothing we can do about it. In fact we can. One of the most famous stories of peace at Christmas involves the series of unofficial and spontaneous ceasefires in the First World War that broke out along the Western Front in 1914.

In the week leading up to 25th December, French, German and British soldiers put their rifles down and crossed trenches to share food and exchange seasonal greetings. In some cases joint **carol** singing and football matches occurred. The 'powers that be' on both sides decided that it should never be repeated – and it never was. But supposing the spark of peace that broke out that Christmas had spread? Might the appalling and largely pointless horror of the First World War – and the Second World War that followed – have been avoided?

So let's enjoy peace at Christmas but let's use the opportunity to give it too.

POLAR BEAR PLUNGE

Christmas attracts more than its fair share of inexplicable and often indefensible pastimes. One of the most bizarre is what is called a Polar Bear Plunge, which involves some form of swimming, mostly in the presence of others, in some Northern Hemisphere river, lake or sea, on or around 25th December or New Year's Day. It's often a good fundraiser for charity.

A Polar Bear Plunge is a great activity to watch on television from the comfort of a warm home!

PRESENTS AND PRESENT GIVING

Christmas is a season associated not just with giving presents but with many diverse rituals around presents, varying according to time-honoured traditions that differ between countries, cultures and even families. One pleasing tradition that heightens

the sense of celebration and anticipation is to put all the presents in one glorious, multicoloured festive pile under the **Christmas tree**.

Present-giving is fascinating: a universal and remarkable act between human beings that builds relationships at every level from families to nations. The **wise men** brought gifts to Jesus at the first Christmas. Let me give you just two verses here:

Thanks be to God for his indescribable gift!
(2 Corinthians 9:15)

For it is by grace you have been saved, through faith – and this is not from yourselves, it is the gift of God – not by works, so that no one can boast. (Ephesians 2:8-9)

As we have been richly given, so we should richly give.

PROPHECY

There is a quote of uncertain origin that 'prediction is very difficult, especially about the future'. Yet if you listen carefully to the words of many Christmas hymns and **carols** and read some of the passages in the gospels, particularly in Matthew, you will hear references to the birth of **Christ** fulfilling prophecy.

Quite a lot of the latter half of what we call the Old Testament, but which Jews saw (and see) as their Bible, is dominated by books called 'prophecies', written by prophets. Yet if we think in terms of prediction of the future, we will be misled. Only a small proportion of the Bible's prophetic literature is actually about the future: the main role of the prophets was to warn and challenge their hearers in the present.

In fact, biblical prophecy covers several things. There are specific predictions (as in 'the **Messiah** will be born in **Bethlehem**') but behind these looms something much larger: the grand, general promises of God's purposes for his people and the world. It is the fulfilling of these great promises that is the most important thing.

If we consider the big promises in our Old Testament, one that follows immediately on from the account of human rebellion that we call 'the Fall', promises that God will send a deliverer, born of a woman, who will crush the head of 'the serpent' who is the devil (**Genesis 3:15**).

Another is the repeated promise to Abraham that his descendants will include one who will be a blessing to the whole world (Genesis 12:3). Still another is that a kingly line will come from the tribe of Judah (Genesis 49:10). That promise is later refined: the great king David is given a prophecy that one of his offspring will be a still greater and even eternal king (2 Samuel 7:12-13).

Around this figure – the Messiah – cluster many other forward-looking statements. Isaiah is full of prophecies, some of which we hear at Christmas, that finally point to a 'servant' who, in some way, will stand in for God's people and bear their punishment for them. Elsewhere there are repeated and wide-ranging promises that the tragic gulf that exists between human beings and God will one day be bridged.

There are 322 prophecies about the Messiah found in the Old Testament that were fulfilled in Jesus – how incredible is that and the reason to celebrate Jesus as the way, the life and the truth.

And let us remember that the story of Jesus is itself not finished. The Old Testament prophecies look forward, not simply to his first coming in humility but his second coming in majesty. The great list of prophecies about all that Jesus is and will do, is only going to be closed when he returns in glorious majesty as King.

REINDEER

The reindeer, known by scientists as *Rangifer tarandus* and by the inhabitants of North America as the caribou, is a large deer with prominent branching antlers that is particularly adapted to cold climates.

During the Ice Age reindeer were found over much of Europe and feature regularly in rock paintings by Stone Age peoples. Currently they are restricted to parts of Greenland, Scandinavia, Russia, Alaska and Canada, where they form large migrating herds. To some extent reindeer have been domesticated, and in Lapland, the very northernmost part of Scandinavia, reindeer are central to the culture of the Lap people, providing them with meat, milk, hair for weaving, hides to make tents and clothing, and horn for tools.

Reindeer are, of course, linked with **Santa Claus** and pull his sleigh; this association explains why Santa is said to live in Lapland. It has been claimed that this link goes back to the Norse god Woden, who rode through the sky with reindeer and forty-two huntsmen. Perhaps, but the main association between reindeer and Santa Claus is barely 200 years old and goes back to an American illustrated children's poem.

Of the wealth of Christmas reindeer stories, two have near universal recognition. One is that of Rudolph the Red-Nosed Reindeer, who originated in a story written in the United States in 1939. In this, a reindeer with the seeming liability of a glowing red nose finds out that this equips him well for being the leading reindeer, especially on foggy nights. Given the fact that these were post-Prohibition days where widespread concern about alcohol abuse remained and many drunkards had red noses, there were doubts about the wisdom of the story. Nevertheless, the risk of publishing was taken and the story proved to be an outstanding success.

A second addition to the legend is that Santa's reindeer bear names and the following are generally accepted: Dasher, Dancer, Prancer, Vixen, Comet, Cupid, Donner and Blitzen. Rudolph is often added as the ninth.

ROBIN

The robin is one of the few birds that, at least in Britain, you can safely assume that everybody can identify. The European robin (the American robin is very different), with its scientific name of *Erithacus rubecula*, is a small songbird of the thrush family with an orange breast. A traditional name for the robin in English is 'Robin Redbreast', a name that reflects the curiosity that, until the arrival of oranges in Europe in the 16th century, the colour we now call 'orange' was considered as a form of red.

Male and female robins look identical and both possess the bright orange breast. They sing throughout most of the year and, unlike most other birds, are largely unafraid of human beings. In fact, they can often be found hunting for food in the soil right next to a working gardener.

Along with **snowmen** and holly, robins have increasingly become popular as 'neutral symbols' for the Christmas festivities.

ROYAL CHRISTMAS MESSAGE

It's very hard not to still think of this as 'The Queen's Speech', an event that was central to many people's Christmas from 1952 until 2021. This Christmas Day broadcast by the reigning monarch of the United Kingdom to the nation and the Commonwealth is a relatively recent addition to Christmas traditions, but no less important for that.

The first such Christmas speech by a British monarch was in 1932 when King George V addressed the nation and the then Empire by the relatively novel technology of radio. The broadcast, written by the celebrated author Rudyard Kipling, was formal and sent from a study in Sandringham House, Norfolk, to be transmitted globally through what was then the Empire Service (now the World Service). The King's Speech soon became an essential part of Christmas, and under George VI played an important part during the Second World War in building the confidence of the nation and the Empire at a time when its very survival was in doubt.

On her accession to the throne, Queen Elizabeth II took over the tradition and made her first broadcast in 1952. In 1957 she began using the newly popular medium of television. A reluctant public speaker who preferred to record her message in advance, the Queen soon made the Christmas address very much her own and allowed it to become much more personal. It was widely observed that, with time, the Queen increasingly let her own Christian faith quietly shine through. King Charles III will, inevitably, be a different monarch, but the continuation of the royal message is almost certainly guaranteed.

SAINT NICHOLAS

Nicholas was born during the 3rd century AD in what is now Turkey. Although we know little of him, it is clear that he was a Christian, was extremely generous and, while still a young man, was made a bishop. He may have been tortured for his faith and is supposed to have died around 343 on 6th December, his feast day.

There are many stories about Nicholas, some of which relate his kindness to individuals and children. One celebrated story is how he came secretly at night to a house to provide money so that three poor daughters could afford to get married.

Nicholas is supposed to have performed miracles, some of them at sea, and became the patron saint of sailors. More importantly, from the point of view of Christmas, he also became the patron saint of children due to his generosity and concern for the young. Today, children in Russia, parts of Belgium, the Netherlands and Germany, receive their Christmas stockings or a small gift on the saint's feast day, 6th December. During the Reformation, which treated the whole idea of saints and saints' days with suspicion, gift-giving shifted to 24th or 25th December to focus children's attention on **Christ** rather than Saint Nicholas. Saint Nicholas, however, proved hard to get rid of and remained widely popular, particularly in Holland.

SAINT STEPHEN

With Saint Stephen, whose feast is celebrated on 26th December, we have a biblical figure. Stephen appears in the early part of the Acts of the Apostles where, in **Acts 6:1-6**, we read how he was one of seven men appointed to ensure that aid was fairly distributed amongst the members of the rapidly growing new church. Stephen appears to have been far more than simply a church administrator and is described as a man 'full of faith and of the Holy Spirit' **(Acts 6:5)** and someone who, 'full of God's grace and power, performed great wonders and signs among the people' **(Acts 6:8)**. Almost inevitably, Stephen faced opposition and was brought to trial before the Jewish religious court, the Sanhedrin. There, as recorded in **Acts 7:54-60**, he met bitter hostility and without a formal verdict was stoned to death in AD 36.

Possibly on the grounds that if you consider Jesus was the first martyr then Stephen was the second, he was allocated a feast day on 26th December, the second day of Christmas. The **carol** 'Good King Wenceslas' refers to this in the words, 'Good King Wenceslas looked out, on the feast of Stephen.'

SANTA CLAUS (FATHER CHRISTMAS)

First a clarification: although the name 'Santa Claus' is used globally, 'Father Christmas' remains popular in Great Britain, but he and Santa Claus are the same. Santa is increasingly a central figure in seasonal festivities so let me write first about 'the man and the legend'.

Two things merged in the 16th century to help create the modern Santa Claus. One was the celebration of **Saint Nicholas,** a figure whose feast day fell on 6th December, as a nocturnal giver of gifts for children. The other was the individual known as 'Father Christmas', a large jovial man in green or scarlet fur-lined robes who stood for good cheer, peace, joy, food, wine and fun.

This individual is known from the time of Henry VIII, who might have made an ideal Father Christmas had he not had such unjovial habits as executing wives and church officials. Soon Saint Nicholas and Father Christmas became inseparably merged.

With the increasing European colonisation of North America the legend evolved. The many Dutch migrants to America brought with them traditions including that of Saint Nicholas and 'Sinter Nikolaas', which soon morphed into 'Sinterklaas' and then 'Santa Claus'. A further addition came from German settlers of the 'Christkind', an angelic child sent by Jesus to bring gifts to good children. (One offshoot of this was the creation of the merry gift-bringer Kris Kringle, who these days is very much the same person as Santa Claus or Father Christmas.)

In the 20th century, the image of Santa Claus began to change, particularly in the United States. Increasingly he became a large individual, bulky, with a beard and rosy cheeks. He acquired **reindeer**, a base near the North Pole or Lapland, and a global, present-giving mission. Although it's claimed that the modern image of Santa Claus with his distinctive red and white clothing, black boots and a beaming red-cheeked face are due to his appearance in Coca-Cola adverts, he was actually depicted in a similar fashion before that. Nevertheless, it's undeniable that Santa's appearance in soft-drink advertising cemented his image in the popular imagination.

With time, Santa has undergone various makeovers and additions. Although in the first part of the 20th century Santa made toys by hand, he soon acquired numerous elves to work for him on some sort of assembly line and, more recently, he seems to have become less a toy manufacturer than a distributor of toys. He also acquired a wife in Mrs Claus, although she rarely features on the European side of the Atlantic.

The idea that children can write to Santa Claus is also relatively novel, as is the idea that he has the mysterious and somewhat disconcerting ability – hitherto only belonging to God – of knowing which children are good or bad. Not all these additions to the Santa Claus legend work comfortably together. So, for example, his claimed ability to descend chimneys seems at odds with his substantial and increasingly expanding waistline.

Whether as Santa Claus or Father Christmas, the jolly man in red has appeared in numerous films and has become something of the ultimate icon of the Christmas season.

SHEPHERDS

Although they occur in different gospels, the **wise men** and the shepherds act as dramatic opposites. Matthew's wise men are outsiders: exotic, wealthy Gentiles who, even if they are not in fact 'kings', are of a social level such that they can meet with a monarch like Herod. In contrast, Luke's shepherds are local, poor, Jewish and humble.

Sheep occur throughout the Bible and in the parched lands of the Middle East, along with goats, they were (and remain) the main livestock animals. Sheep provided wool, milk, meat and leather and, as sacrificial animals, could command a high price. In fact, it's possible that the sheep being raised at **Bethlehem** were destined for temple sacrifices; if so, the idea in John 1:29 that Jesus was 'the Lamb of God, who takes away the sins of the world' would have a special significance.

In Bible times every family might be expected to have at least a few sheep and wealthy farmers could have flocks running into the hundreds (see Luke 15:1-7). Sheep, however, need managing. Lacking both intelligence and survival skills they are prone to falling from cliffs, dying of thirst and being eaten by lions and wolves. They are also easily stolen. The vulnerability of sheep has always required shepherds, often with defensive weapons and sometimes with dogs.

The life of a shepherd was hard and unpleasant. The constant need to find fresh pastures in arid lands meant constant travel and vigilance. Not only that, but the necessity of having to deal with all the uncomfortable and distasteful aspects of animal management made them both physically and ritually unclean. In every way, shepherds got their hands dirty. The life of a shepherd put them very much on the margins of Jewish society.

Yet if shepherds were considered as outsiders, they were not entirely viewed in a negative way. Theirs was a valued role and there was also a recognition that the relationship between sheep and shepherds had deep parallels between that of human beings – equally inclined to wander off – and God. After all, **Psalm 23** speaks of God being our shepherd, and the greatest of the Jewish kings, David, had started life as a shepherd.

The fact that shepherds were both at the bottom and on the edge of 'decent society' doubtless appealed to Luke. In his gospel and its successor volume, the Acts of the Apostles, we read how, with the good news of Jesus, God reaches out to the lowly and the outsiders. Nothing has changed.

SNOW

At least in the Northern Hemisphere, Christmas is associated with snow but, in fact, that association is more one of tradition and sentiment than reality. Snowy Christmases are actually rare in most parts of Britain. According to the Met Office, for most parts of the United Kingdom Christmas comes at the beginning of the period when it's likely to snow. In the 18th and 19th centuries, colder climates meant that snow at Christmas was more common. The change from the Julian to the Gregorian calendar in 1752 is also a factor as it brought 25th December forward by nearly two weeks.

Something that is very definitely a piece of Christmas trivia is the formal definition of a white Christmas by the British Met Office: it is one snowflake to be observed falling in the 24 hours of 25th December somewhere  in the UK. A more reasonable definition of a white Christmas is where 'more than 40 per cent of stations in the UK reported snow on the ground at 9am' but this has only occurred four times since 1960 – in 1981, 1995, 2009 and 2010. With climate change, the probability of a white Christmas will surely be further reduced.

One or two Christmas songs talk about snow and frost at **Bethlehem**. The most famous of these is 'In the Bleak Midwinter' by the fine Victorian poet Christina Rossetti; a work that distinguishes itself from most other Christmas songs and hymns by the twin virtues of being genuinely profound and deeply poetic. This is the first verse.

In the bleak midwinter, frosty wind made moan,
Earth stood hard as iron, water like a stone;
Snow had fallen, snow on snow, snow on snow,
In the bleak midwinter, long ago.

This has often been subject to popular criticism because 'as we all know' Bethlehem is in the Middle East and thus always baking hot. In fact, it's at nearly 800 metres (2,600 feet) and snow is not unknown in winter. I suspect, too, that Rossetti is using poetic imagery to describe not simply the state of the weather but the cold state of the human heart.

The Bing Crosby version of the song 'White Christmas' is one of the great phenomena of the music industry and is considered to be the world's best-selling single. Written by Irving Berlin in 1940, it was first performed on Christmas Day 1941, just weeks after the attack on Pearl Harbour had brought America into the Second World War. With its nostalgic and even melancholic recall of happier and quieter times, it spoke deeply to many during the war. It is credited with selling fifty million copies.

SNOWMEN

Linked with **snow** is the snowman, a figure traditionally made from two large snowballs in the UK and three in the USA. Various decorations are added for the face, most famously a carrot for the nose.

There have been various famous portrayals of snowmen. An early one was Frosty the Snowman who appeared in a 1950s Christmas song. The animated film *The Snowman*, based on a wordless children's picture book by Raymond Briggs, has become something of a Christmas regular in the UK, and the song from the film, 'Walking in the Air', has become a classic. Significantly, although the original book made no reference to Christmas, this was brought into the film.

It's a great film but its poignant tone of the inevitability of things melting away is in fact very much the opposite of the Christmas message of eternal hope.

'STIR-UP' SUNDAY

Traditionally, 'Stir-Up' Sunday was when a **Christmas pudding** was made, five weeks before Christmas. It owes its name to the fact that in the *Book of Common Prayer* of the Church of England, used from the 16th to the mid-20th centuries, the collect – a special prayer – for that day, reads as follows:

> Stir up, we beseech thee, O Lord, the wills of thy faithful people; that they, plenteously bringing forth the fruit of good works, may by thee be plenteously rewarded; through Jesus Christ our Lord. Amen.

The first phrase of this prayer neatly coincided with the tradition that Christmas puddings should be made four to five weeks before Christmas, a process that involved a great deal of stirring. In some families 'Stir-Up' Sunday involved everybody stirring the pudding mix and, as each person took their turn, they made a wish.

STOCKINGS

As with so much at this season, no one is completely certain how stockings became involved with Christmas. One story looks back to **Saint Nicholas**. Having decided to fund three penniless young women so that they could get husbands, he is supposed to have come at night and thrown coins down the chimney, which were caught in the stockings that were hanging to dry over the fireplace.

Whatever the origin, Christmas stockings are still regularly hung up by children on **Christmas Eve** for **Father Christmas**, or someone, to fill with presents.

TINSEL

One element of **Christmas decorations** is that of tinsel: thin, flexible strips of shiny metallised plastic foil. Tinsel reflects light – the word comes from the Old French '*estincele*', meaning 'to spark' – and so has the effect of multiplying the impact of Christmas **lights**.

One rather charming legend about tinsel is that in the 17th century, a widow was left with several children to raise and had to work very hard to support them. She created a festive **Christmas tree** to greet the children on Christmas Day but lamented that she could not afford decorations for it. During the night spiders spun webs through the limbs of her tree and when she woke on Christmas morning and pulled back the curtains to let sunlight in, the sun's rays struck the webs so they gleamed and glittered.

TURKEY

A North American game bird, turkeys were brought over to Europe in the 1520s and soon replaced peacock, swan and wild boar as the main meat at **Christmas dinner**, although goose remained commonly eaten until well into Victorian times.

This replacement by turkey was probably due to several things, including **Charles Dickens**' influential popularisation of a turkey dinner in ***A Christmas Carol***.

Turkeys are relatively easy to raise and put on weight rapidly. The result of this is that they are one of the cheapest ways of producing large amounts of high-quality meat, something that is important if you have got an entire extended family sitting hungrily around the table at Christmas. The fact that a turkey is easy to carve is probably also a factor. Nevertheless, turkey is not the easiest of meats to cook and can be much less moist than other poultry, such as chicken or duck.

The demand for turkeys at Christmas is extraordinary and some years have seen well over ten million consumed in the UK alone.

TWELVE DAYS OF CHRISTMAS AND TWELFTH NIGHT

Although for many of us Christmas has been reduced to one or two days of food and family snatched from our allotted yearly holidays, there is a tradition of a longer, more leisured festive season, famously referred to as 'the twelve days of Christmas'.

In 567 the Council of Tours in France proclaimed the twelve days from Christmas to Epiphany as a sacred and festive season. The twelve days soon took on more than just a religious significance. Allegedly beginning with King Alfred the Great and continuing into Tudor times, this period became a compulsory national holiday in Britain. All work, except for looking after animals, ceased, restarting again on the first Monday after Twelfth Night. Although a holiday of this length may seem difficult to imagine today, at a time when most people worked on the land, an extended winter break was possible.

Within the twelve days there were – and are – a number of church festivals. There is the feast of **Saint Stephen** on the 26th and the feast of Saint John the Evangelist on the 27th. I've always assumed that Saint John was to be celebrated for writing a gospel, three letters and the Book of Revelation, but in popular thinking he seems to have been more acclaimed for having miraculously drunk a glass of poisoned wine without ill effect. As a result, on the 27th it was quite common for the faithful to bring bottles of wine or cider to church to be blessed at Mass. This was then consumed no doubt in the ritual of **wassailing**.

December 28th was *Childermas*, or the Holy Innocents' Day, which commemorated the massacre of young children in **Bethlehem** by **Herod the Great**.

The twelve days of Christmas are celebrated in the seasonal song of the same name, which catalogues the progressive giving of often bizarre gifts over the period. After twelve verses the final list is:

A partridge in a pear tree,
Two turtle doves,
Three French hens,
Four calling birds,
Five gold rings,
Six geese a-laying,
Seven swans a-swimming,
Eight maids a-milking,
Nine ladies dancing,
Ten lords a-leaping,
Eleven pipers piping,
Twelve **drummers drumming**.

The song was first recorded in 1780 and, with countless versions, has become widespread. Attempts have been made to try and find a deep meaning to the words but no satisfactory explanation has been produced.

UGLY JUMPERS

One of the fascinating features of Christmas is that it is continually evolving; some traditions fade away while new ones are created.

One relatively recent addition to the catalogue of Christmas curiosities is that of the 'Ugly Christmas Jumper'. In this self-explanatory tradition, individuals wear over-the-top, colourful and often unappealing pullovers in the run-up to Christmas, frequently with clashing patterns or tasteless images. Some people even hold Ugly Jumper Parties.

On a more positive note, however, in the UK Christmas Jumper Day has become an annual fundraising event held in early December, with the proceeds going to the charity Save the Children.

VIRGIN BIRTH

The idea that Jesus was born from a virgin without a human father is widely termed the 'virgin birth'.

The virgin birth is an essential part of traditional Christian theology. The basis for the belief that Jesus was conceived in Mary through the action of the Holy Spirit is declared in **Matthew 1:18-25** and **Luke 1:26-38**. The two clear mentions in Matthew and Luke are, however, significant, not least because their nativity accounts clearly come from separate and different sources. Both make several things clear. Mary, a virgin who is engaged to be married to Joseph of the line of David, will conceive a child without sexual intercourse, simply through the power of the Holy Spirit. Matthew claims that this fulfils a passage in **Isaiah 7:14**:

> **Therefore the Lord himself will give you a sign: the virgin will conceive and give birth to a son, and will call him Immanuel.**

The belief in the virgin birth is present in all the creeds of every traditional or historic church.

WASSAILING

'Wassailing' is one of those words heard almost exclusively at Christmas and which very few people really know the meaning of. It has very ancient origins: a 'wassail' was a toast for good health at festivities, especially during **Christmas Eve** and **Twelfth Night**. The word comes from the Saxon greeting *'waes hail'* meaning 'be in good health' and as such is similar to the English 'cheers!' or the French *'santé'*.

In Anglo-Saxon times, drinking, like eating, was more than just a matter of responding to bodily appetites. It was something that helped build bonds of trust between communities and individuals in a volatile age when violence was often never very far away; taking in alcohol often prevented the shedding of blood.

So important was a wassail that special bowls were made for it, and sometimes a particular brew of ale mixed with eggs, spices, honey, cream and roasted apples. Sometimes pieces of toasted bread were put on the top of the drink, and here it is claimed is the origin of the expression 'to make a toast'.

Wassailing seems to have evolved into a variety of drinking traditions at Christmas time. So, for instance, in some situations, poor people would go round to the households of the wealthy with a filled wassail bowl and, after singing **carols**, they would ask for hospitality, a gift, food or money in return for a taste from the wassail bowl. In other situations, carollers would expect to be rewarded with a hot, spiced (often cider-based) drink, known as a 'wassail'.

WISE MEN (MAGI, THREE KINGS)

In any nativity play, the arrival of the three exotic, gift-bearing individuals to the **crib** is often the highlight of the drama. Traditionally referred to as the three 'kings' or the three 'wise men', many Bibles will in fact term these men 'Magi', which a footnote will probably explain as 'wise men' or even 'astrologers'.

The Greek word 'magos', which comes from Old Persian 'magus', 'powerful', is used for astrologers: influential advisers who would guide decision-making in the ancient world.

With respect to the biblical account, the reality is that the information we have about these fascinating individuals is very limited. They are only mentioned in **Matthew 2** and there only briefly.

> After Jesus was born in Bethlehem in Judea, during the time of King Herod, Magi from the east came to Jerusalem and asked, 'Where is the one who has been born king of the Jews? We saw his star when it rose and have come to worship him.' (Matthew 2:1-2)

> Then Herod called the Magi secretly and found out from them the exact time the star had appeared. He sent them to Bethlehem and said, 'Go and search carefully for the child. As soon as you find him, report to me, so that I too may go and worship him.' After they had heard the king, they went on their way, and the star they had seen when it rose went ahead of them until it stopped over the place where the child was. When they saw the star, they were overjoyed. On coming to the house, they saw the child with his mother Mary, and they bowed down and worshipped him. Then they opened their treasures and presented him with gifts of gold, frankincense and myrrh. And having been warned in a dream not to go back to Herod, they returned to their country by another route. (Matthew 2:7-12)

It's a dramatic account and one that makes you wish we knew more. It is generally recognised that the Magi were some sort of astrologers. The fact that the word 'astrologer' is shunned in most translations is because the Bible is negative about astrology as a practice for God's people.

But where were the Magi from? The 'east' could cover an enormous area and suggestions have been made of Persia (modern Iran), India or even China. Linked with this is the question of how much the Magi knew about what we call the Old Testament and its promises of a **Messiah**. Jewish communities existed in Mesopotamia and Persia so there may have been some knowledge of their hope of a coming Messiah.

Today there are a rapidly growing number of Iranian Christians and they may be fascinated to know that the great explorer Marco Polo (1254–1324) claimed to have visited the tombs of the wise men in Saveh, a city south of Teheran.

We are not told the number of the Magi nor that they are kings. The assumption that there were three is rooted in the three gifts: gold, frankincense and myrrh. This, along with their regal role, is cemented in popular consciousness by the **carol** 'We Three Kings of Orient Are'.

Gold is a gift that speaks of authority and kingship and is perfectly suitable for one who was indeed to be the 'King of kings'.

Frankincense is the dried resin of the Boswellia tree, which at the time of Jesus grew in Arabia, India, Somalia and Ethiopia. Preparing the resin was a time-consuming process, which made frankincense a very expensive perfume. Frankincense was used in temple worship and Christians have seen it as foreshadowing the priestly ministry of **Christ**, the one who was, in one person, the ultimate high priest, sacrifice and temple. Frankincense is used as incense, a symbol of prayer and communion with God.

Myrrh is a gum resin that oozes from cuts made in small, thorny Commiphora trees found in Africa and Arabia. When the waxy myrrh hardens it is usually made into powder. Myrrh was used in funeral preparations and embalming and would have been amongst the spices that the body of Jesus was wrapped with. It is often taken as pointing towards Christ's atoning death on the cross.

Whatever their intentions at the beginning of their journey, when the wise men saw the infant Jesus 'they bowed down and worshipped him' (Matthew 2:11). Although they were no doubt expecting an infant in some kind of noble palace surrounded by servants, they were nevertheless able to see in this infant, hidden in the poverty, something of God's divine glory.

Despite its brief appearance in the gospels, the visit of the Magi was very important in early Christianity, particularly outside the Jewish world. So, for example, at least eighty-five paintings of the visit of the Magi have been identified in the Roman catacombs associated with Christian worship and burial. The reason for this seems easy to understand: Gentile Christians looked on the Magi as the forerunners of those who, like themselves, had come to believe in Jesus from outside the Jewish faith. Indeed, they may well have taken pride in the way the Gentile Magi recognised Jesus as the Messiah before the Jews did.

It is likely that early Christians saw in the account of the Magi, the fulfilment of various Old Testament prophecies. Here are three.

Nations will come to your light and kings to the brightness of your dawn . . . Herds of camels will cover your land, young camels of Midian and Ephah. And all from Sheba [Ethiopia] will come, bearing gold and incense and proclaiming the praise of the LORD. (Isaiah 60:3,6)

May the kings of Tarshish and of distant shores bring tribute to him. May the kings of Sheba and Seba [probably Yemen] present him with gifts. May all kings bow down to him and all nations serve him. (Psalm 72:10-11)

This is what the LORD says – the Redeemer the Holy One of Israel – to him who was despised and abhorred by the nation, to the servant of rulers: 'Kings will see you and stand up, princes will see and bow down, because of the LORD, who is faithful, the Holy One of Israel, who has chosen you.' (Isaiah 49:7)

By AD 250, the popular account of the Magi was already being substantially embellished. They were three in number and they had been given names: Gaspar (or Caspar), Melchior and Balshasar (or Balthazar). Soon it was assumed that they were three *kings*. A further elaboration of this came with the notion that the kings were from different areas: Gaspar from India, Melchior from Persia and Balthazar from Arabia.

Still later, as exposure to different races grew in Europe, it became common to imagine these kings as representing the peoples of the world, with one white (often represented as old), one black and another with Asiatic features. This multi-racial aspect of the wise men has long been shown in nativity plays.

The three kings became venerated as saints and martyrs and their supposed relics were transferred from Constantinople (modern Istanbul) to Milan and from there to Cologne Cathedral in the 12th century.

Devotion to the Magi was especially fervent in the Middle Ages, where they became the patron saints of travellers.

Putting aside all the traditions, the wise men are well worth reflecting on. In Matthew's gospel they are clearly seen as precursors of the many Gentiles who will come to faith in Christ.

They also foreshadow the Great Commission to the disciples at the end of Matthew's gospel, with its command for believers in Jesus to go into the whole world and proclaim the good news of Christ.

There is also a personal message in these wise men to those who are considering Christ. Despite their evident wealth and status, these individuals were very much outsiders to the world of the Jewish faith with all its hopes of a Messiah. Yet despite this, and with very limited information, they rose up and journeyed to find for themselves the one who would be the King of the Jews and possibly even more than that. Jesus is well worth coming a long way for.

WREATHS

One of the most prominent signs that we are in the Christmas season is the presence of wreaths – rings of flowers, evergreen foliage and red ribbons – hung on the doors of houses or inside over fireplaces or doorways.

Like so much of the Christmas season, wreaths have a long history going back to ancient Persia and Greece. Often the context there was that of celebration and even today you get victory wreaths in sporting and other contests. Conquering generals and powerful rulers often wore a wreath and were frequently depicted bearing one in images and sculptures.

XMAS

The origin of the abbreviation of Xmas is fairly straightforward. The Greek word for **Christ** is 'Χριστος' or '*Christos*' and begins with the letter *chi*, which looks identical to our X.

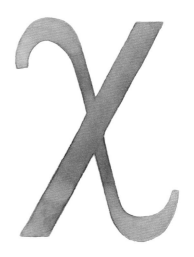

The shortening of Christmas in records has been common practice for a millennium. I suppose you could argue that Xmas was 'textspeak' half a millennium before the smartphone. A key point, however, is that although we may write Xmas as an abbreviation it should *never* be used in spoken language.

YULE LOG

Long before the Christianisation of Western Europe, it was common at midwinter for a large log to be ceremonially laid on a fire amid various rituals. Sometimes the Yule log was the only element of light and heat allowed in a house, and in other traditions a piece of the Yule log was preserved in order to light the next year's log.

Behind this seems to be the way that certain trees were considered sacred and their burning had some sort of spiritual significance. Shorn – at least openly – of its traditional significance, the traditional burning of the Yule log continued well into the Middle Ages and beyond.

Its decline in recent centuries probably reflects nothing more than the fact that it requires a large and open fireplace, something that is becoming rare except in very old houses.

Linked with the burning of the Yule log, and still popular, is the creation of an edible miniature version. Most versions of these Christmas logs are an elaborate Swiss roll, sometimes soaked with alcohol and often covered in chocolate, and decorated to resemble a log of wood.